SOLVED QUESTION PAPERS OF LL.B. IV SEMESTER

CCS UNIVERSITY, MEERUT

PROF. (DR.) GOVIND PRASAD GOYAL AND PROF. ADARSH VERMA |
ADVOCATE | SUPREME COURT OF INDIA

This Book

is

Dedicated

To

Future Legal Craftsmen

Contents

Foreword

It is with great pleasure and enthusiasm that I introduce this invaluable resource, "Solved Question Papers of LL.B. IV Semester of CCS University," meticulously crafted by Prof. (Dr.) Govind Prasad Goyal and Prof. Adarsh Verma, Advocate, Supreme Court of India.

Legal education forms the bedrock of a just and equitable society, shaping the minds and skills of future legal practitioners, policymakers, and guardians of justice. Amidst the rigors of legal academia, one often finds solace and guidance in well-constructed study materials, especially those that offer a glimpse into the examination patterns and expectations.

In this compendium, Prof. Goyal and Prof. Verma have curated a comprehensive collection of solved question papers tailored specifically for the LL.B. IV Semester curriculum of CCS University. Their years of academic expertise and practical legal experience have been distilled into these pages, offering students a roadmap to navigate through the complexities of legal examinations.

Each solved question serves not only as a test of knowledge but also as a platform for understanding the intricate nuances of legal reasoning, interpretation, and application. Aspiring lawyers will find within these pages a treasure trove of insights, strategies, and techniques honed through years of dedication and scholarly pursuit.

Moreover, the inclusion of answers with detailed explanations elevates this work beyond a mere compilation of questions. It becomes a dynamic learning tool, fostering deeper comprehension and critical thinking among students.

Prof. Goyal and Prof. Verma's commitment to academic excellence and their passion for legal education shine through in this endeavor. Their dedication to empowering the next generation of legal minds is evident, and this resource stands as a testament to their unwavering resolve to nurture and guide aspiring lawyers.

I have no doubt that students, educators, and legal professionals alike will find immense value in the insights offered within these pages. It is my sincere hope that this compendium serves as a beacon of knowledge and inspiration for all who embark on the journey of legal learning.

Warm regards,
Prof. (Dr.) Bhavish Gupta
HoD-Law
IMS Law College, Noida

Preface

Welcome to the compilation of Solved Question Papers for LL.B. IV Semester of CCS University. This book is meticulously crafted to serve as a comprehensive resource for students embarking on their journey through the intricate landscape of legal studies.

Law is not merely a subject; it's a dynamic field that intersects with every aspect of our society. As aspiring legal professionals, it is imperative to understand the nuances of legal principles, precedents, and practices. These solved question papers are designed to aid students in their preparation for examinations by providing insight into the patterns, formats, and types of questions commonly encountered in LL.B. IV Semester examinations.

Each solved question paper included in this book has been meticulously curated and presented to offer clarity, understanding, and practical application of legal concepts. By delving into these papers, students can familiarize themselves with the examination environment, develop effective strategies for time management, and enhance their problem-solving skills.

It is essential to acknowledge the diligent efforts of educators, scholars, and legal experts whose contributions have enriched the content of this book. Their dedication to fostering excellence in legal education is reflected in the quality and depth of the material presented here.

As you embark on this academic journey, remember that success is not merely defined by the marks you obtain but by the knowledge, understanding, and skills you acquire along the way. Use this book as a tool to hone your legal acumen, cultivate critical thinking abilities, and strive for academic excellence.

We extend our best wishes to all the students undertaking the LL.B. IV Semester examinations. May this book serve as a valuable companion in your quest for legal knowledge and proficiency.

Happy studying!

Authors

Acknowledgements

We extend our sincerest gratitude and heartfelt appreciation to all the students, colleagues, and practitioners who contributed to the creation of the "Solved Question Papers of LL.B. IV Semester of CCS University." Your invaluable dedication, expertise, and collaborative spirit have made this endeavor possible.

To the students who diligently provided feedback, insights, and assistance throughout the process, thank you for your unwavering support and commitment to excellence. Your active involvement has enriched the quality and relevance of the solved question papers, ensuring their effectiveness as a valuable resource for academic preparation.

We also express our deepest appreciation to our esteemed colleagues for their guidance, encouragement, and continuous support. Your wisdom, expertise, and constructive feedback have been instrumental in shaping the content and structure of the solved question papers, enhancing their educational value and utility.

Furthermore, we extend our gratitude to the practitioners whose real-world experience and insights have enriched the solved question papers with practical relevance and applicability. Your contributions have bridged the gap between theory and practice, enriching the learning experience for students and fostering a deeper understanding of legal concepts and principles.

Together, your collective efforts have culminated in the creation of a comprehensive and reliable resource that will undoubtedly benefit students, educators, and practitioners alike. Your dedication to advancing legal education and scholarship is truly commendable, and we are deeply grateful for your invaluable contributions.

Thank you once again for your unwavering commitment, support, and collaboration. Your contributions have made a meaningful difference and will continue to inspire and empower future generations of legal professionals.

With heartfelt appreciation,

Authors

Prologue

In the labyrinthine corridors of legal academia, where the pursuit of justice intertwines with the intricacies of the law, lies a repository of knowledge, both revered and formidable. Among the countless tomes that line the shelves of aspiring lawyers, one treasure shines brightly — the solved question papers of LL.B. IV Semester of CCS University.

Within these pages dwell the echoes of countless minds grappling with the complexities of legal theory and practice. Each question, each answer, is a testament to the diligence and dedication of those who have walked this path before. They are not merely ink on paper but milestones marking the journey towards legal enlightenment.

From the hallowed halls of the classroom to the solitude of late-night study sessions, these solved question papers have been a beacon of guidance for generations of law students. They are more than just a collection of queries and solutions; they are a bridge between theory and application, between aspiration and achievement.

As the pages turn, a narrative unfolds — a narrative of challenges met, obstacles overcome, and knowledge gained. Here, in the crucible of examination, minds are sharpened, ideas are tested, and futures are forged. Each question paper is a chapter in the ongoing saga of legal education, a testament to the pursuit of excellence in the noble profession of law.

So, let us delve into this treasury of wisdom, let us navigate its passages with curiosity and reverence. For within these solved question papers lie not only the keys to academic success but also the seeds of legal acumen and the promise of a brighter tomorrow in the realm of jurisprudence.

Disclaimer

The solved question papers provided herein for LL.B. IV Semester of CCS University have been meticulously crafted by Prof. (Dr.) Govind Prasad Goyal and Prof. Adarsh Verma, Advocate, Supreme Court of India, with the intention of aiding students in their academic endeavors. However, it is essential to note that these solved papers are intended for educational purposes only and should not be construed as official examination papers or substitutes for studying the prescribed curriculum.

While every effort has been made to ensure the accuracy and reliability of the content presented, no guarantee is made regarding the completeness, correctness, or suitability for any particular purpose. Users are encouraged to verify the information provided herein and utilize these solved papers as supplementary study materials alongside their regular course materials.

Furthermore, neither Prof. (Dr.) Govind Prasad Goyal nor Prof. Adarsh Verma, Advocate, Supreme Court of India, assume any liability for any errors, omissions, or damages arising from the use of these solved papers. Users are solely responsible for their interpretation and application of the information contained herein.

By accessing and utilizing these solved question papers, users acknowledge and agree to the terms of this disclaimer.

CHAPTER ONE

Company Law

2023 Question Paper

Q.1. What do you mean by public company?

Ans. In the Indian legal regime, a public company is defined under the Companies Act, 2013. Here's what constitutes a public company in India:

- Minimum Number of Members: A public company must have a minimum of seven members/shareholders.
- Minimum Number of Directors: It must have a minimum of three directors.
- Share Capital: There is no restriction on the maximum amount of share capital for a public company. It can raise capital from the public by issuing shares.
- Transferability of Shares: The shares of a public company are freely transferable, subject to certain provisions of the Articles of Association of the company and compliance with securities laws.
- Disclosure Requirements: Public companies have more stringent disclosure requirements compared to private companies. They are required to comply with various reporting and disclosure norms prescribed by the Securities and Exchange Board of India (SEBI) and other regulatory authorities.
- Listing Requirements: If a public company intends to offer its shares to the public, it must comply with the listing requirements of the stock exchanges where it intends to list its shares.
- Minimum Subscription: A public company must receive a minimum subscription for its shares before it can commence its business operations.
- Public Offering: Public companies can issue shares to the public through initial public offerings (IPOs) or follow-on public offerings (FPOs) to raise capital for business expansion, investment, or other purposes.
- Compliance Obligations: Public companies are subject to more regulatory oversight and compliance obligations compared to private companies. They must adhere to corporate governance standards and file periodic reports with regulatory authorities.

To summarize, a public company in the Indian legal regime is a corporate entity that offers its shares to the public and is subject to stringent regulatory requirements to protect the interests of investors and ensure transparency and accountability in its operations.

Q.2. What do you mean by the prospectus of the company?

Ans. In the context of the Companies Act, 2013, a prospectus is a legal document issued by a company to invite the public to subscribe for its shares or debentures. The Companies Act, 2013 defines a prospectus and lays down regulations regarding its contents, format, and issuance. Here's what it entails:

- Definition: According to Section 2(70) of the Companies Act, 2013, a prospectus is defined as "any document described or issued as a prospectus and includes any notice, circular, advertisement or other document inviting deposits from the public or inviting offers from the public for the subscription or purchase of any shares in, or debentures of, a body corporate."

- Contents: The prospectus must contain all material information about the company, its promoters, directors, financial statements, objects, and any other information that may influence investors' decisions. This includes details about the company's business, management, financial performance, risks involved, terms of the issue, and any other information required by the regulatory authorities.
- Format and Presentation: The prospectus must be prepared and presented in a clear, concise, and comprehensible manner. It should be divided into sections and sub-sections for easy reference, and the information provided must be accurate, truthful, and not misleading.
- Approval and Filing: Before issuing the prospectus to the public, it must be approved by the board of directors of the company. In certain cases, such as public offerings, it may also require approval from regulatory authorities like the Securities and Exchange Board of India (SEBI). Additionally, the prospectus must be filed with the Registrar of Companies (RoC) and other relevant regulatory authorities.
- Liability: Any misstatement or omission in the prospectus can lead to legal liabilities for the company, its directors, promoters, and other parties involved in its preparation and issuance. Investors who suffer losses due to false or misleading information in the prospectus may have legal recourse against the company and its officers.

Overall, the prospectus serves as a vital document for investors to make informed decisions about investing in the company's shares or debentures. It ensures transparency, accountability, and investor protection in the capital market ecosystem.

Q.3. What do you mean by debentures as per The Companies Act 2013?

Ans. As per the Companies Act, 2013, debentures are a form of long-term debt instrument issued by companies to raise funds from the public or institutional investors. Here's what debentures entail under the Companies Act, 2013:

- Definition: Section 2(30) of the Companies Act, 2013 defines debentures as "debenture" includes debenture stock, bonds or any other instrument of a company evidencing a debt, whether constituting a charge on the assets of the company or not.
- Nature of Instrument: Debentures represent a loan agreement between the company issuing them (the issuer) and the investors (debenture holders). They are a form of debt financing for the company and entitle the holders to a fixed rate of interest and repayment of the principal amount at maturity.
- Types of Debentures:
- - Secured Debentures: These are backed by specific assets or properties of the company, providing security to the debenture holders in case of default.
- - Unsecured Debentures: Also known as 'naked debentures,' these are not backed by any collateral and rank lower in terms of priority in case of liquidation or default.
- Terms and Conditions: The terms and conditions of debentures, including interest rate, repayment terms, conversion rights (if any), and redemption provisions, are specified in the debenture trust deed or prospectus issued by the company.
- Issue and Redemption: Companies issue debentures through public offerings or private placements, subject to regulatory approvals. Debentures may be redeemable (repaid) on maturity or may be irredeemable (perpetual). Companies may also offer convertible debentures, which can be converted into equity shares at a later date.
- Register of Debenture Holders: Companies are required to maintain a register of debenture holders, recording details such as names, addresses, and holdings of debentures. This register must be kept at the registered office of the company and is open for inspection by debenture holders and regulatory authorities.
- Debenture Trustees: In case of secured debentures, companies are required to appoint debenture trustees to protect the interests of debenture holders. The debenture trustee represents the debenture holders and ensures compliance with the terms of the debenture trust deed.
- Legal Status: Debentures represent a contractual obligation of the company to repay the principal amount and interest to the debenture holders. Failure to fulfill this obligation may result in legal action against the company by the debenture holders.

Overall, debentures are an important source of long-term financing for companies, providing flexibility in raising funds while offering investors a fixed income investment option.

Q.4. What is the effect of the certificate of incorporation according to the Companies Act 2013?

Ans. According to the Companies Act, 2013, the certificate of incorporation has significant effects on a company. Here's what it entails:

- Legal Existence: The certificate of incorporation signifies the creation of a separate legal entity distinct from its shareholders. Once a company is incorporated and the certificate is issued by the Registrar of Companies (RoC), the company comes into existence as a legal entity capable of conducting business activities.
- Corporate Identity: The certificate of incorporation provides the company with a unique corporate identity, including its name and registration number. This identity distinguishes the company from other entities and allows it to enter into contracts, own property, sue, and be sued in its own name.
- Limited Liability: Shareholders of a company enjoy limited liability, meaning their liability is limited to the amount unpaid on their shares. The certificate of incorporation confirms this limited liability protection, shielding shareholders from personal liability for the company's debts and obligations.
- Capacity to Contract: With the issuance of the certificate of incorporation, the company gains the legal capacity to enter into contracts and undertake business activities. It can engage in various transactions, including buying and selling goods, hiring employees, and entering into agreements with third parties.
- Perpetual Succession: A company enjoys perpetual succession, meaning its existence is not affected by changes in its membership. The certificate of incorporation ensures that the company continues to exist notwithstanding changes in shareholders or directors.
- Transferability of Shares: Shareholders can freely transfer their shares in the company, subject to any restrictions imposed by the company's articles of association or applicable laws. The certificate of incorporation confirms the transferability of shares and facilitates the trading of securities in the company.
- Regulatory Compliance: The certificate of incorporation signifies that the company has complied with the statutory requirements for incorporation under the Companies Act, 2013. It confirms that the company has fulfilled the necessary formalities, including submission of documents, payment of fees, and compliance with regulatory provisions.

To conclude, the certificate of incorporation under the Companies Act, 2013, confers legal recognition and status to a company, enabling it to operate as a separate legal entity with limited liability and capacity to engage in business activities.

Q.5. What do you mean by holding company and subsidiary company ?

Ans. As per the Companies Act, 2013, a holding company and subsidiary company are defined based on their relationship and ownership structure. Here's what each term means:

- Holding Company

- A holding company, also known as a parent company, is a company that controls another company, known as its subsidiary, by owning a majority of its voting shares or exercising significant influence over its management.
- Under Section 2(46) of the Companies Act, 2013, a holding company is defined as a company that holds the majority of shares in another company, thereby controlling its management and operations.
   - Characteristics of a holding company include:
   - Holding voting rights in its subsidiary company, allowing it to control the subsidiary's decisions.
   - Having the ability to appoint or remove directors of the subsidiary.
   - Exercising influence over the financial and operational policies of the subsidiary.

- Subsidiary Company:

- A subsidiary company is a company that is controlled by another company, known as its holding company. The holding company owns a majority of the subsidiary's voting shares or has significant influence over its management.

- Under Section 2(87) of the Companies Act, 2013, a subsidiary company is defined as a company in which the holding company controls the composition of the board of directors or exercises control over more than half of the total voting power.

- Characteristics of a subsidiary company include:

- Being controlled by a holding company through ownership of a majority of voting shares or exercising significant influence over management.

- Operating independently but under the strategic direction and control of the holding company.

- Having its own separate legal identity and obligations, despite being controlled by the holding company.

To conclude, a holding company is a company that controls another company (its subsidiary) by owning a majority of its shares or exercising significant influence over its management. A subsidiary company is a company that is controlled by another company (its holding company) and operates under its strategic direction and control. These relationships are crucial in corporate structures and have legal implications in terms of governance, financial reporting, and liability.

Q.6. Discuss about the kinds of share-capital.

Ans. According to the Companies Act, 2013, share capital can be classified into various types, each with its own characteristics and rights. Here are the kinds of share capital as per the Companies Act, 2013:

Equity Share Capital:

- Equity shares represent ownership in a company and entitle the shareholders to voting rights and dividends. They carry residual rights in the company, meaning they have a claim on the company's assets and profits after all other obligations are met.

- Equity shareholders participate in the company's growth and success through capital appreciation and dividends, but they also bear the risk of losses if the company performs poorly.

- Equity shares do not carry any fixed rate of dividend and are considered the riskiest form of investment among different types of shares.

2. Preference Share Capital:

- Preference shares are a type of share capital that carries preferential rights over equity shares with respect to dividends and repayment of capital.

- Preference shareholders are entitled to receive a fixed rate of dividend before any dividend is paid to equity shareholders. However, they do not usually have voting rights or carry limited voting rights.

- Preference shares can be further classified into various types based on their features, such as cumulative preference shares (where unpaid dividends accumulate), non-cumulative preference shares, participating preference shares (entitled to additional dividends beyond the fixed rate), and redeemable preference shares (redeemable at a specified future date).

3. Authorized Share Capital:

- Authorized share capital refers to the maximum amount of share capital that a company is authorized to issue as per its memorandum of association.

- It represents the total value of shares that a company can legally offer to the public or issue to its shareholders. Companies often set their authorized share capital at a higher amount than their actual capital requirements to provide flexibility for future fundraising.

- Authorized share capital can be increased or decreased by following the prescribed procedures under the Companies Act, 2013.

4. Issued Share Capital:

- Issued share capital refers to the portion of authorized share capital that a company has actually issued or allotted to shareholders.

- It represents the total value of shares that have been issued and subscribed by shareholders, and it may be equal to or less than the authorized share capital.

- Issued share capital can be increased through the issuance of new shares or decreased through share buybacks or cancellation of shares, subject to compliance with legal requirements.

5. Paid-up Share Capital:

- Paid-up share capital refers to the portion of issued share capital that shareholders have actually paid for and settled with the company.

- It represents the amount of capital contributed by shareholders towards the company's operations and investments.

- Paid-up share capital may be equal to or less than the issued share capital, depending on the extent to which shareholders have paid for their shares.

These are the main kinds of share capital recognized under the Companies Act, 2013, providing companies with flexibility in raising capital and shareholders with varying rights and preferences based on their investment preferences and risk appetite.

Q.7. Discuss the disqualifications of the director.

Ans. According to the Companies Act, 2013, certain disqualifications exist that prevent individuals from being appointed or continuing as directors of a company. These disqualifications are designed to ensure that individuals serving as directors meet certain criteria of integrity, competence, and eligibility. Here are some of the key disqualifications of directors under the Companies Act, 2013:

1. Undischarged Insolvency: An individual who has been declared as an undischarged insolvent by a court is disqualified from being appointed as a director of a company.

2. Unsound Mind: Individuals who are of unsound mind and have been declared as such by a competent court are disqualified from serving as directors.

3. Conviction for Offenses: Individuals who have been convicted by a court of any offense involving moral turpitude and sentenced to imprisonment for a period of six months or more, and a period of five years has not elapsed from the date of expiration of the sentence, are disqualified.

4. Conviction for Certain Offenses under Companies Act: Individuals who have been convicted of offenses under the Companies Act, such as fraud or mismanagement, and sentenced to imprisonment for at least six months, are disqualified for a period of five years from the date of release.

5. Failure to Pay Calls or Repay Deposits: Individuals who have failed to pay any calls in respect of any shares of the company held by them, or have failed to repay any deposits accepted by the company, are disqualified from being appointed as directors of any other company.

6. Disqualification by Regulatory Authorities: Individuals who have been disqualified by any regulatory authority, such as the Securities and Exchange Board of India (SEBI) or the Reserve Bank of India (RBI), from being appointed as directors of a company are disqualified.

7. Non-compliance with Director Identification Number (DIN): Directors who do not have a valid Director Identification Number (DIN) or whose DIN has been deactivated due to non-compliance with regulatory requirements are disqualified.

8. Disqualification by National Company Law Tribunal (NCLT): The National Company Law Tribunal has the authority to disqualify directors if they are found to be involved in fraudulent activities or acts prejudicial to the interests of the company.

9. Non-resident Directors: Non-resident individuals may also be subject to disqualifications if they fail to comply with certain residency requirements prescribed under the Companies Act, 2013

It's important for companies and individuals to be aware of these disqualifications to ensure compliance with the law and maintain the integrity of corporate governance practices. Directors who are disqualified may face legal consequences and restrictions on their ability to serve on the board of directors of a company. Additionally, companies must conduct proper due diligence before appointing individuals as directors to ensure that they do not fall under any of the disqualifications mentioned above. Compliance with these disqualifications helps uphold the principles of corporate governance, transparency, and accountability within the corporate sector.

Q. 8. What do you mean by the doctrine of Ultra-vires?

Ans. The doctrine of Ultra Vires, as per the Companies Act, 2013, refers to the principle that limits the powers of a company to those activities and objectives that are explicitly stated in its memorandum of association. The term "Ultra Vires" is a Latin phrase meaning "beyond the powers."

Key aspects of the doctrine of Ultra Vires under the Companies Act, 2013 include:

1. Memorandum of Association (MoA): The MoA of a company outlines the objects for which the company is formed and the powers it can exercise to achieve those objects. Any act done by the company beyond the scope of its MoA is considered Ultra Vires.

2. Doctrine of Constructive Notice: The doctrine of Ultra Vires is based on the principle of constructive notice, which implies that anyone dealing with the company is deemed to have knowledge of its MoA. Therefore, third parties dealing with the company are expected to ensure that the company's actions fall within the ambit of its MoA.

3. Void Acts: Any action taken by a company that is Ultra Vires is considered void and cannot be ratified by the company, even if all shareholders agree. This is because the company lacks the legal authority to undertake such actions.

4. Exceptions: While the doctrine of Ultra Vires limits the powers of a company to its MoA, there are certain exceptions:

- Acts undertaken for the benefit of the company's business that are reasonably incidental or ancillary to its main objects are considered intra vires (within the powers).

- Acts authorized by the company's articles of association or subsequently ratified by a special resolution of the shareholders may also be valid.

5. Legal Implications: The consequences of Ultra Vires acts include:

- The company may be restrained from carrying out such acts through legal injunctions sought by shareholders or regulatory authorities.

- Directors or officers of the company who authorize Ultra Vires acts may be personally liable for any losses incurred by the company or third parties as a result of such actions.

Overall, the doctrine of Ultra Vires serves to ensure that companies operate within the legal framework prescribed by their MoA, thereby protecting the interests of shareholders, creditors, and other stakeholders, and maintaining the integrity of corporate governance.

Q.9. What do you mean by company ? What are the types of company? What is the difference between a private company and a public company?

Ans. A company, in a legal sense, is an entity formed under the law to engage in business activities. It is a separate legal entity from its owners (shareholders) and can own property, enter into contracts, sue, and be sued. There are various types of companies, but broadly, they can be categorized into:

1. Sole Proprietorship: A business owned and operated by a single individual. The owner is personally liable for all debts and obligations of the business.

2. Partnership: A business owned and operated by two or more individuals who share profits and liabilities.

3. Corporation: A legal entity separate from its owners. Corporations can be further divided into:

- Private Limited Company: Also known as a private company, it is owned by a small group of shareholders and does not offer its shares to the public. It is often denoted by "Pvt Ltd" in its name.

- Public Limited Company: Also known as a public company, it offers its shares to the public and is listed on a stock exchange. It is often denoted by "Ltd" in its name.

The differences between a private company and a public company are regulated by laws such as the Companies Act. In the case of India, as per the Companies Act 2013, some of the key differences between private and public companies include:

1. Minimum number of members: A private company must have a minimum of two members, while a public company must have a minimum of seven members.

2. Maximum number of members: A private company can have a maximum of 200 members, excluding employees and past employees who are also members. There is no maximum limit on the number of members for a public company.

3. Transferability of shares: In a private company, the transfer of shares is restricted, and the consent of other shareholders is usually required. In a public company, shares are freely transferable.

4. Minimum subscription: A public company must receive a minimum subscription amount for its shares before it can start its business, whereas a private company doesn't have such requirements

5. Issue of prospectus: A public company must issue a prospectus or file a statement in lieu of a prospectus before it can issue shares to the public. A private company is not required to issue a prospectus.

6. Number of directors: A private company must have a minimum of two directors, while a public company must have a minimum of three directors.

These are some of the key differences between private and public companies as per the Companies Act 2013 in India.

Q.10. What is "the doctrine of indoor management?"

Ans. The doctrine of indoor management is a legal principle that serves as a corollary to the doctrine of constructive notice in company law. It essentially protects outsiders dealing with a company from the consequences of any irregularities or internal irregularities that might exist within the company's internal management structures.

Here's an explanation of the doctrine of indoor management as per the Companies Act 2013:

1. Doctrine of Constructive Notice: Under company law, outsiders dealing with a company are generally deemed to have knowledge of the company's constitutional documents (such as its memorandum and articles of association) and any resolutions or proceedings that are publicly available. This is known as the doctrine of constructive notice.

2. Exceptions with the Doctrine of Indoor Management: However, the doctrine of indoor management provides an exception to the doctrine of constructive notice. It recognizes that it is impractical for outsiders to have knowledge of all internal matters of a company. Therefore, if an outsider is dealing with a company in good faith, they can assume that internal company procedures have been followed, even if this is not actually the case.

3. Protection of Outsiders: The doctrine of indoor management essentially protects outsiders who are dealing with a company in good faith. If an outsider enters into a transaction with a company, they can rely on the external manifestations of authority, such as the company's public documents and representations by officers, directors, or agents, even if there are irregularities in the company's internal management.

For instance, if a person enters into a contract with a company and the contract is signed by someone who appears to have authority, the outsider can assume that this person has the authority to bind the company, even if there are internal irregularities, such as a lack of proper authorization according to the company's internal rules.

Thus we can say that the doctrine of indoor management protects outsiders who deal with a company in good faith by allowing them to rely on the external manifestations of authority, even if there are internal irregularities or breaches of internal procedures within the company. It's an important principle that balances the need for legal certainty with the practical realities of business dealings.

Q.11. Discuss the rule of lifting of the corporate veil in detail.

Ans. The "lifting of the corporate veil" is a legal principle that allows courts to disregard the separate legal personality of a corporation and look behind the corporate structure to hold its shareholders or directors personally liable for the actions or obligations of the corporation. This principle is invoked in exceptional circumstances where it is deemed necessary to prevent injustice or fraud. The concept is particularly relevant in company law and is applied in various jurisdictions around the world. Here's a detailed discussion of the rule of lifting the corporate veil:

1. Separate Legal Personality: One of the fundamental principles of company law is that a corporation has a separate legal personality distinct from its shareholders, directors, and officers. This means that the corporation can enter into contracts, own property, sue, and be sued in its own name. Shareholders, directors, and officers are generally not personally liable for the debts and obligations of the corporation beyond their investment in the company.

2. Purpose of the Corporate Veil: The concept of separate legal personality encourages investment and entrepreneurship by providing limited liability protection to shareholders and directors. It allows individuals to invest in companies without risking their personal assets beyond their investment in the company.

3. Exceptions to Separate Legal Personality:

- Statutory Exceptions: There are certain statutory provisions that explicitly provide for the lifting of the corporate veil in specific circumstances. For example, in cases of fraudulent trading, where a company carries on business with intent to defraud creditors, the courts may disregard the separate legal personality of the company.

-Common Law Exceptions: Apart from statutory exceptions, courts have developed common law principles to lift the corporate veil in certain situations. These include cases of fraud, improper conduct, evasion of legal obligations, and where the company is used as a mere façade or sham to conceal the true nature of transactions.

4. Grounds for Lifting the Corporate Veil:

- Fraud: One of the most common grounds for lifting the corporate veil is fraud. If the corporate structure is used to perpetrate fraud or deceive creditors, courts may disregard the separate legal personality of the company and hold the individuals behind the company personally liable.

- Agency: If the company is deemed to be an agent or alter ego of its shareholders or directors, courts may lift the corporate veil to hold those individuals personally liable for the company's actions or obligations.

- Public Interest: In certain cases involving matters of public interest or public policy, courts may lift the corporate veil to prevent injustice or ensure compliance with the law.

5. Discretionary Nature: It's important to note that the decision to lift the corporate veil is at the discretion of the courts and is based on the specific facts and circumstances of each case. Courts will consider factors such as the nature of the wrongdoing, the degree of control exercised by the individuals, and the extent to which justice demands intervention.

6. Limitations and Caution: While the doctrine of lifting the corporate veil serves an important role in ensuring accountability and preventing abuse of the corporate form, courts are generally reluctant to do so and will only intervene in exceptional cases where there is clear evidence of wrongdoing or injustice. Moreover, the principle should be applied cautiously to avoid undermining the legitimate purposes of limited liability and separate legal personality.

To sum up, the rule of lifting the corporate veil is a legal doctrine that allows courts to pierce the corporate veil and hold shareholders or directors personally liable for the actions or obligations of a corporation in exceptional circumstances. It serves to prevent abuse of the corporate form and ensure accountability, but courts exercise discretion and apply the principle cautiously, considering the specific facts and circumstances of each case.

Q.12. What do you mean by the winding of the company and what are the grounds for winding up of the company?

Ans. The winding up of a company, also known as liquidation, refers to the process of bringing a company's existence to an end. This involves selling off its assets, paying off its debts, and distributing any remaining assets to its shareholders or creditors according to their respective rights. The winding-up process can be initiated voluntarily by the company itself (voluntary winding up) or by an order of the court (compulsory winding up).

Under the Companies Act 2013 in India, there are various grounds for winding up a company, which can be classified into two main categories: voluntary winding up and compulsory winding up. Here's an overview of the grounds for winding up as per the Companies Act 2013:

1. Voluntary Winding Up:

- Resolution: The company may pass a special resolution to wind up voluntarily if it decides that it cannot continue its business due to financial difficulties, operational issues, or any other reason.

- Expiration of Period or Occurrence of Event: If the company was formed for a specific period or a particular purpose and that period expires or the purpose is achieved, the company may wind up voluntarily.

- Special Circumstances: The company may wind up voluntarily if it resolves to do so by a special resolution for any reason it deems fit.

2. Compulsory Winding Up:

- Inability to Pay Debts: If the company is unable to pay its debts, it may be wound up by the court. This occurs when a creditor, or creditors collectively, files a petition for winding up due to the company's inability to pay its debts.

- Just and Equitable Grounds: The court may order the winding up of a company on "just and equitable" grounds. This can occur in various situations, such as deadlock among shareholders, oppression of minority shareholders, or where it is no longer feasible for the company to continue operating.

3. Default in Holding Annual General Meeting (AGM): If a company fails to hold its AGM for a continuous period of at least two years, the Registrar of Companies may strike off the name of the company from the register. However, before doing so, the Registrar must send a notice to the company and give it a reasonable opportunity to rectify the default.

4. Failure to Commence Business: If a company does not commence its business within one year of its incorporation or suspends its business operations for a whole year, it can be wound up by the Registrar of Companies.

These are some of the key grounds for winding up a company as per the provisions of the Companies Act 2013 in India. Winding up is a complex legal process that involves various stakeholders, including creditors, shareholders, directors, and regulatory authorities, and it is typically overseen by a liquidator appointed by the court or shareholders.

Q.13. What do you mean by the Board of Directors and what are the powers of the Board of Directors?

Ans. The Board of Directors of a company is a group of individuals elected by the shareholders to oversee the management and strategic direction of the company. The board acts as the governing body of the company and is responsible for making major decisions, setting policies, and ensuring the company's overall success. The Board of Directors typically consists of a mix of executive directors (who are involved in the day-to-day operations of the company) and non-executive directors (who provide oversight and guidance).

Under the Companies Act 2013 in India, the Board of Directors of a company has various powers and responsibilities outlined in the law. Here are some of the key powers of the Board of Directors as per the provisions of the Companies Act 2013:

1. Management and Administration: The Board of Directors has the overall responsibility for managing the affairs of the company and ensuring its proper administration. This includes overseeing the company's operations, finances, and compliance with applicable laws and regulations.

2. Decision Making: The board has the authority to make major decisions on behalf of the company, including decisions related to investments, mergers and acquisitions, divestitures, financing, and strategic planning.

3. Appointment and Removal of Officers: The board has the power to appoint and remove the company's officers, such as the CEO, CFO, and company secretary. The CEO is typically responsible for the day-to-day management of the company and reports to the board.

4. Declaration of Dividends: The board has the authority to declare dividends to the shareholders based on the company's financial performance and available profits. However, dividends can only be declared out of profits or surplus funds of the company.

5. Borrowing Powers: The board has the power to borrow money on behalf of the company, subject to certain limits and conditions prescribed under the law and the company's articles of association.

6. Appointment of Auditors: The board is responsible for appointing the company's auditors and fixing their remuneration. Auditors are responsible for examining the company's financial statements and providing an independent opinion on its financial position and performance.

7. Compliance and Disclosure: The board is responsible for ensuring that the company complies with all applicable laws, regulations, and corporate governance standards. This includes ensuring timely and accurate disclosure of financial information and other material information to shareholders and regulatory authorities.

8.Corporate Governance: The board is responsible for maintaining high standards of corporate governance within the company, including establishing effective internal controls, risk management systems, and ethical standards.

These are some of the key powers and responsibilities of the Board of Directors as per the provisions of the Companies Act 2013 in India. The board plays a crucial role in the governance and management of the company, and its effective functioning is essential for the company's long-term success and sustainability.

2022 Question paper

Q.1. Foreign company.

Ans. In accordance with the Companies Act 2013, a foreign company is defined as follows:

A "foreign company" means any company or body corporate incorporated outside India, which:

- Has a place of business in India, whether by itself or through an agent, physically or through electronic mode; and
- Conducts any business activity in India in any other manner.

Under the Companies Act 2013, foreign companies operating in India are subject to certain provisions and regulations, including those related to registration, compliance, and taxation. These provisions are intended to ensure transparency, accountability, and legal compliance for foreign entities conducting business activities within India's jurisdiction.

Q.2. Reconstruction.

Ans. Under the Companies Act 2013, "reconstruction" refers to any transaction involving the transfer of the whole or any part of the undertaking, property, or liabilities of a company to another company. It also includes any consolidation or division of shares, any transfer of shares, or any other arrangement that results in a change in the ownership or control of the company.

The Act provides specific provisions and regulations regarding reconstruction, including the approval process by shareholders and creditors, the role of the National Company Law Tribunal (NCLT), and the rights and obligations of the parties involved. The primary objective of these provisions is to ensure transparency, fairness, and protection of the interests of stakeholders during the reconstruction process.

Q.3. Board Meeting.

Ans. In the context of the Companies Act 2013 in India, a board meeting is a formal gathering of the directors of a company to discuss and decide on various matters pertaining to the business. Here's a more detailed definition:

A board meeting is a meeting of the board of directors of a company, duly convened and conducted in accordance with the provisions of the Companies Act 2013 and the company's Articles of Association. The Act specifies certain requirements and procedures regarding the conduct of board meetings, including the following key points:

Convening the Meeting- The board meeting must be convened by the company secretary or any person authorized by the board for this purpose. Adequate notice must be given to all directors, specifying the date, time, and venue of the meeting, along with an agenda of the matters to be discussed.

Quorum-The Act specifies the minimum number of directors required to be present at a board meeting to constitute a quorum. If the quorum is not present within a certain period after the scheduled start time, the meeting may be adjourned.

Proceedings-The discussions and decisions taken at a board meeting must be recorded in the minutes of the meeting. These minutes should be prepared, maintained, and signed by the company secretary or any other person appointed by the board for this purpose.

Decision Making-Matters requiring the approval of the board, such as financial statements, strategic decisions, appointment of key personnel, etc., are deliberated upon and decided during board meetings.

Compliance-Board meetings must be conducted in compliance with the provisions of the Companies Act 2013, the company's Articles of Association, and any other applicable laws or regulations.

Board meetings play a crucial role in the governance and management of a company, as they provide a forum for directors to collectively discuss and make decisions on important matters affecting the company's operations and future direction.

Q.4. Pre-emptive rights.

Ans. Pre-emptive rights, as defined in the Company Act 2013, refer to the rights granted to existing shareholders of a company that allow them to maintain their proportional ownership in the company by having the first opportunity to purchase additional shares of the company before they are offered to outsiders or new investors.

These rights are also known as rights of pre-emption or rights of first refusal.

Under the Company Act 2013, pre-emptive rights are typically outlined in the Articles of Association of a company. The purpose of granting pre-emptive rights is to protect existing shareholders from dilution of their ownership stake when the company issues new shares. By providing existing shareholders with the opportunity to purchase additional shares in proportion to their existing holdings, pre-emptive rights ensure that they can maintain their proportional ownership and voting rights in the company.

If a company intends to issue new shares, it must first offer those shares to existing shareholders in proportion to their existing holdings, typically at a price determined by the board of directors or through a shareholder resolution. Only if existing shareholders decline to exercise their pre-emptive rights can the company then offer the new shares to outsiders or new investors.

Pre-emptive rights help promote fairness and protect the interests of existing shareholders by allowing them to participate in future equity issuances on equal terms with new investors. These rights also help maintain stability and continuity in the ownership structure of the company.

Q.5. Dissolution.

Ans. In the context of the Companies Act, 2013, dissolution refers to the formal process by which a company ceases to exist as a legal entity. Dissolution can occur for various reasons, such as:

Voluntary Dissolution: This occurs when the members or shareholders of a company decide to wind up its affairs voluntarily. It typically involves passing a special resolution in a general meeting, followed by filing necessary documents with the Registrar of Companies (RoC).

Compulsory Dissolution: This occurs under circumstances mandated by law, such as:

- Failure to commence business within one year of incorporation.

- Inability to carry on business for a period exceeding one year.

- By order of the Tribunal or Registrar of Companies in case of default or non-compliance with statutory requirements.

Dissolution by Tribunal: The National Company Law Tribunal (NCLT) has the authority to order the dissolution of a company on various grounds, including oppression and mismanagement, or if it's found to be carrying on activities prejudicial to public interest or national security.

Dissolution through Liquidation: This is the process of selling off a company's assets, paying off creditors, and distributing any remaining assets to shareholders before formally dissolving the company.

Once a company is dissolved, it ceases to exist as a legal entity, and its name is struck off from the register maintained by the Registrar of Companies. After dissolution, any assets remaining with the company are distributed among its creditors and members according to the provisions of the law.

Q.6. Discuss the facts and decision of Salomon v. Salomon and Co. Ltd. Case.

Ans. "Salomon v. Salomon & Co. Ltd." is a landmark case in UK corporate law that established the principle of corporate personality and limited liability. Here's a discussion of the facts and decision of the case:

Facts:

In 1892, Mr. Salomon, a successful leather merchant, incorporated a company called Salomon & Co. Ltd. He was the principal shareholder and held 20,001 of the company's 20,007 shares. His wife and five children each held one share. Mr. Salomon sold his business to the newly formed company for £39,000, of which £10,000 was paid in cash and the balance in debentures and shares. The company also issued debentures to Mr. Salomon, secured by a floating charge over the company's assets.

However, the company faced financial difficulties and went into liquidation. The liquidator argued that the company was a mere facade, and Mr. Salomon was personally liable for the company's debts.

Decision:

The House of Lords unanimously ruled in favor of Mr. Salomon. Lord Halsbury, in his judgment, emphasized the separate legal personality of the company. He stated that once the company was properly incorporated, it becomes a distinct legal entity from its shareholders. Therefore, the liabilities of the company are separate from those of its shareholders.

This case established the principle of corporate personality, which means that a company is considered a legal person in its own right, capable of entering contracts, owning property, and being sued. Additionally, the case confirmed the concept of limited liability, meaning that shareholders are generally not personally liable for the debts of the company beyond their investment in the company.

Significance:

"Salomon v. Salomon & Co. Ltd." is considered a foundational case in corporate law. It laid the groundwork for modern corporate structures by establishing the principle of separate legal personality and limited liability. This principle has since become a fundamental aspect of corporate law not only in the UK but also in many other jurisdictions around the world. It has enabled the growth of commerce and investment by providing a framework that encourages entrepreneurship while mitigating personal financial risk for shareholders.

Q.7. What is the appointment of independent directors made by the company?

Ans. The appointment of independent directors by a company refers to the process by which individuals who are considered independent of the company's management and operations are selected and appointed to serve on the company's board of directors. Independent directors play a crucial role in providing oversight, strategic guidance, and accountability within the company.

Here's how the process typically works:

Identification and Selection: The company's nominating or governance committee, often composed of existing board members, identifies potential candidates for independent director positions. These candidates are typically individuals with expertise, experience, and integrity who can bring diverse perspectives to the board.

Evaluation and Qualification: The nominating committee evaluates the qualifications of potential candidates, considering factors such as their professional background, industry knowledge, independence from the company (including financial independence), and any potential conflicts of interest.

Appointment: Once suitable candidates have been identified and vetted, the board of directors formally appoints them as independent directors through a resolution or vote. Shareholders may also need to approve the appointment, depending on the company's bylaws and regulatory requirements.

Onboarding and Orientation: Newly appointed independent directors undergo an onboarding process to familiarize themselves with the company's operations, culture, governance structure, and strategic objectives. This may include orientation sessions, meetings with key executives, and access to relevant documentation and resources.

Ongoing Responsibilities: Independent directors are expected to actively participate in board meetings, committees, and strategic discussions. They provide independent oversight, challenge management's decisions, and represent the interests of shareholders. They also may serve on various board committees, such as audit, compensation, and nominating committees, to fulfill specific oversight responsibilities.

Continued Evaluation: Independent directors' performance and effectiveness are periodically evaluated by the board or its committees to ensure they continue to meet the company's evolving needs and governance standards.

Overall, the appointment of independent directors is crucial for ensuring transparency, accountability, and effective corporate governance within a company, thereby safeguarding the interests of shareholders and stakeholders.

Q.8. Doctrine of indoor management is an exception to the doctrine of constructive notice. as per Companies Act 2013..Discuss.

Ans. The doctrine of indoor management is indeed an exception to the doctrine of constructive notice, particularly in the context of the Companies Act 2013 in India. To understand this, let's first define both doctrines:

Constructive Notice: According to this doctrine, anyone dealing with a company is deemed to have notice of all the provisions of the company's memorandum and articles of association. In simpler terms, it implies that persons dealing with a company are expected to have read and understood the company's constitutional documents, and they are bound by the contents therein.

Doctrine of Indoor Management: This doctrine, also known as the Turquand's rule, provides protection to outsiders who enter into transactions with a company. It states that those dealing with a company from the outside are entitled to assume that internal procedures prescribed by the company's constitution have been duly complied with. In other words, outsiders are not bound to inquire into the regularity of internal proceedings of a company.

Now, let's discuss how the doctrine of indoor management serves as an exception to the doctrine of constructive notice:

- Protecting External Parties: While the doctrine of constructive notice primarily protects the company and its internal operations by ensuring that outsiders are aware of the company's constitutional documents, the doctrine of indoor management primarily protects external parties who are dealing with the company. It recognizes that outsiders cannot reasonably be expected to know the internal workings of a company, and thus, they should be protected when they rely on the apparent authority of officers or the regular conduct of business.

- Reliance on Apparent Authority: Under the doctrine of indoor management, external parties are entitled to assume that officers of the company have the authority to act on behalf of the company in the ordinary course of business. This means that even if the internal rules of the company have not been followed, outsiders can still enforce contracts entered into with the company if they acted in good faith and without knowledge of any irregularities.

- Balancing Interests: The doctrine of indoor management strikes a balance between the interests of the company and the interests of outsiders. While the doctrine of constructive notice protects the company's internal affairs, the doctrine of indoor management ensures that external parties are not unfairly prejudiced by internal irregularities or failures to follow internal procedures.

Let us conclude that, the doctrine of indoor management acts as an exception to the doctrine of constructive notice by protecting external parties who transact with a company in good faith, even if the company's internal procedures have not been followed. This doctrine serves to balance the interests of the company and external parties, ensuring fairness and efficiency in commercial dealings.

Q.9. Discuss the civil and criminal liability for misstatement in the prospectus as per Companies Act 2013.

Ans. Discuss the civil and criminal liability for misstatement in the prospectus as per Companies Act 2013.

Ans. Under the Companies Act 2013 in India, the prospectus is a vital document for public offerings of securities issued by a company. It provides crucial information to potential investors to help them make informed decisions about investing in the company. Misstatements or inaccuracies in the prospectus can have serious legal consequences, both civil and criminal, for the company and its directors. Here's an overview:

Civil Liability:

a. Liability of the Company: If the prospectus contains any untrue statement, the company issuing the prospectus is liable to pay compensation to anyone who subscribes for securities on the faith of the prospectus and suffers a loss. This means that if an investor relies on false information in the prospectus and suffers financial loss as a result, they can sue the company for compensation.

b. Liability of Directors: Directors of the company are also held personally liable if the prospectus contains any untrue statement. They can be sued for damages by any person who subscribes for securities based on the false information in the prospectus and suffers loss as a result. Directors can be held liable even if they were unaware of the misstatement, as they have a duty to ensure the accuracy of the prospectus.

c..Defenses: Directors can defend themselves against civil liability if they can prove that they had reasonable grounds to believe, and did believe, that the statement was true, or that the statement was immaterial, or that they withdrew their consent to the prospectus and gave reasonable public notice of the withdrawal before the issue of the securities.

Criminal Liability:

a. Penalties for Misstatements: If any person, including the company or its directors, knowingly issues a prospectus containing any untrue statement, they can be held criminally liable. The penalty may include imprisonment for a term which may extend to two years or with fine which may extend to Rs. 50 lakh (or both).

b.Fraudulent Activities: In cases where the misstatement in the prospectus is a result of fraudulent activities, the penalties can be more severe. Individuals involved in fraudulent activities related to the prospectus issuance may face imprisonment for a term which may extend to 10 years and shall also be liable to fine which shall not be less than the amount involved in the fraud but may extend to three times the amount involved in the fraud.

It's important for companies and their directors to ensure that the prospectus contains accurate and truthful information to avoid civil and criminal liability. This underscores the importance of due diligence in the preparation and issuance of prospectuses in order to protect investors and maintain the integrity of the capital markets.

Q.10. Reduction in share capital made with or without the approval of the Tribunal as per Companies Act 2013. Comment.

Ans. In accordance with the Companies Act 2013, a reduction in share capital can be carried out either with the approval of the Tribunal or without it, depending on the circumstances and the method chosen by the company. Let's explore both scenarios:

Reduction with Tribunal Approval:

When a company decides to reduce its share capital with the approval of the Tribunal, it needs to follow a specific process outlined in the Companies Act. This typically involves filing a petition with the National Company Law Tribunal (NCLT) or Regional Director, depending on the jurisdiction, seeking approval for the reduction. The company needs to provide justification for the reduction and demonstrate that it will not adversely affect the interests of creditors or shareholders.

The Tribunal will review the petition, consider objections if any, and then issue an order approving the reduction if it deems it appropriate. Once the Tribunal's approval is obtained, the company can proceed with implementing the reduction as per the terms specified in the order.

Reduction without Tribunal Approval:

The Companies Act also provides certain methods through which a company can reduce its share capital without the need for Tribunal approval. These methods include:

- Buyback of shares: The company can buy back its own shares from shareholders, subject to compliance with the provisions of the Act, including the requirement of passing a special resolution and meeting other conditions.

- Extinguishment of liability on shares not taken up: If any shares are not taken up or accepted by shareholders, the company can extinguish the liability on such shares without requiring Tribunal approval.

- Forfeiture of shares: If shares are forfeited due to non-payment of calls or any other reason specified in the articles of association, the company can reduce its share capital by the amount of the forfeited shares without Tribunal approval.

In both cases, whether reduction with or without Tribunal approval, it's crucial for the company to adhere to the provisions of the Companies Act and fulfill all legal requirements to ensure the reduction is carried out lawfully and in the best interests of the company and its stakeholders. Additionally, the company should consider consulting legal and financial professionals to navigate the process effectively.

Q.11.Discuss with exceptions the rule propounded in the case of Foss v. Harbottle.

Ans. "Foss v. Harbottle" is a landmark case in English corporate law that established the rule known as the "rule in Foss v. Harbottle." This rule essentially states that where a wrong has been done to a company, the proper plaintiff to bring an action in court is the company itself and not the individual shareholders, unless certain exceptions apply.

Exceptions to the rule in Foss v. Harbottle include:

Derivative actions: Shareholders may bring a derivative action on behalf of the company when the company itself fails to take action against wrongdoers within the company. This allows shareholders to sue on behalf of the company to redress wrongs done to it.

Ultra vires actions: If the company's actions are beyond its legal powers as defined in its memorandum of association, individual shareholders may bring a claim to restrain the company from undertaking such actions.

Personal rights/actions: Shareholders can sue if their personal rights have been infringed, such as where the majority has used their voting power to oppress the minority or where the shareholders' agreement has been breached.

Fraud on the minority: Shareholders may bring an action if the majority shareholders have committed fraud or acted unlawfully, causing harm to the minority shareholders.

Wrongdoer control: If the wrongdoers are in control of the company, such as cases of director misconduct, it may be impractical or futile to expect the company to take legal action, and therefore individual shareholders may have standing to sue.

These exceptions recognize situations where it would be unjust or impractical to require the company itself to bring an action, and thus allow individual shareholders to seek legal remedies. They provide safeguards against abuse of power by the majority and ensure that minority shareholders have recourse to the courts to protect their interests.

Q.12. In what circumstances, lifting of corporate veil is done as per the Companies Act, 2013 ?

Ans. In accordance with the Companies Act 2013 in India, the lifting of the corporate veil is a legal concept that allows courts to disregard the separate legal personality of a company and look at the individuals behind it, typically in situations where there is an abuse of the corporate form or where justice demands it. The veil may be lifted under certain circumstances:

Fraud or improper conduct: If a company is formed or used for fraudulent purposes or to perpetrate a fraud, courts may lift the corporate veil to hold the individuals involved personally liable for their actions.

Agency or trustee relationship: When the company is acting as an agent or trustee for its members or shareholders, it becomes necessary to look beyond the company's separate legal personality to establish the rights and liabilities of those involved.

Group companies: In cases involving a group of companies, where one company is merely a façade for another within the group or where there is an attempt to evade legal obligations or exploit the corporate form unfairly, courts may lift the veil to ensure justice.

Alter ego: If it can be shown that the company is essentially the alter ego of its shareholders or directors, with no real separation between the company and its owners, courts may disregard the corporate entity and hold the individuals personally liable.

Public interest: In situations where it is necessary to prevent the misuse of the corporate form for illegal or unethical purposes that are against public interest, courts may lift the veil to hold those responsible accountable.

It's important to note that the decision to lift the corporate veil is made by the courts on a case-by-case basis, and each situation will be evaluated based on its own merits and the specific circumstances involved.

Q.13. What are the producer companies? What is the purpose of a producer's company?

Ans. A producer company is a type of business entity that primarily focuses on agricultural production, procurement, processing, and marketing of primary produce (agricultural goods) of its members. These companies are governed by the Indian Companies Act, 2013, and are formed by farmers, agriculturists, and individuals engaged in the production of primary produce.

The primary purpose of a producer company is to facilitate the socio-economic development of its members, who are typically small-scale farmers or producers. Here are some key objectives and purposes of producer companies:

Collective Bargaining Power: By pooling resources and collective bargaining, producer companies aim to secure better prices for their produce and reduce the dependency on middlemen.

Market Access:Producer companies often assist their members in accessing markets directly, eliminating intermediaries and ensuring fair prices for their products.

Capacity Building:They provide training and education to their members to enhance agricultural practices, improve productivity, and ensure quality standards.

Access to Finance:Producer companies can facilitate access to credit and finance for their members, enabling them to invest in farming inputs, equipment, and infrastructure.

Value Addition: They may engage in processing, packaging, and value addition activities to enhance the value of agricultural produce before entering the market, thus increasing profitability for their members.

Legal Protection: Producer companies provide legal protection and recognition to small-scale farmers and producers, ensuring their rights and interests are safeguarded.

Promotion of Cooperatives:Producer companies promote the cooperative movement by encouraging collaboration and mutual support among members, fostering a sense of community and solidarity.

Thus, the purpose of a producer company is to empower farmers and producers, improve their livelihoods, and contribute to the sustainable development of rural areas by leveraging collective action and resources.

2019 Question Paper

Q.1. Forfeiture of shares as per Indian Companies Act 2013.

Ans. Regulations 28 to 34 of Table F of Schedule I of the Companies Act, 2013 outline the procedures for share forfeiture in India. Share forfeiture is a serious measure and must strictly adhere to the company's articles of association. Recent cases, like Bhagwandas Goverdhandas Kedia vs. Girdharilal Parshottamdas & Co, emphasize that forfeiture should be exercised in good faith and for the company's benefit. M/s. Siel Foods & Fertilizer Industries vs. B.S. Atwal underscores shareholders' responsibility in maintaining updated contact details. Hindustan Construction Co. Ltd. vs. S.J. Jain further clarified that forfeiture must follow a fair process and not be influenced by improper motives. Understanding and adhering to these legal principles is crucial in today's corporate climate, where share forfeiture may become more prevalent amid financial challenges.

Q.2. Holding Company.

Ans. According to Section 2(46) of the Companies Act, 2013, a "holding company" refers to a company that has one or more other companies as its subsidiary companies. In essence, a holding company exercises control over its subsidiaries either through ownership of their shares or through other means. This relationship establishes a hierarchical structure within corporate entities, where the holding company typically has significant influence or control over the strategic and operational decisions of its subsidiaries. The Companies Act provides regulations and guidelines governing the relationship between holding and subsidiary companies to ensure transparency, accountability, and proper governance within corporate groups.

Q.3. Prospectus.

Ans. In accordance with Section 2(70) of the Indian Companies Act, 2013, a prospectus embodies a pivotal document for any company seeking public investment. It encompasses various forms such as the red herring prospectus under Section 32 or the shelf prospectus under Section 31. Moreover, it extends to encompass any communication, be it a notice, circular, or advertisement, inviting public offers for subscribing or purchasing securities of a corporate entity. Essentially, it serves as a comprehensive guide, detailing the company's objectives, financial status, risks, and terms of the offering, ensuring transparency and accountability in soliciting investments from the public.

Q.4. Minimum subscription.

Ans. Minimum Subscription, a mandate under the Indian Companies Act 2013, compels companies to secure a specified capital amount during issuance. This requirement shields investors and the company, ensuring a baseline commitment before proceeding with public offerings. Failure to meet the minimum subscription necessitates cancellation of the issue and refunds application deposits within 15 days, safeguarding investor interests. The Act enforces a 90% ceiling limit on capital collection, compelling companies to gather at least 90% of the offered capital. Compliance, monitored by the Registrar of Companies, maintains market integrity and investor confidence while upholding financial viability for companies.

Q.5. One Person Company.

Ans. The One Person Company (OPC) structure under the Companies Act 2013 allows a single individual to establish a corporate entity, enjoying limited liability. It enables entrepreneurs to embark on ventures without the need for partners. The OPC model facilitates easier compliance, with reduced administrative burden compared to traditional corporate structures. The founder assumes both ownership and managerial responsibilities, maintaining autonomy over decision-making. OPCs foster entrepreneurship by providing a platform for solo innovators to operate within a corporate framework. This legal framework promotes small-scale enterprises, contributing to economic growth and encouraging individuals to pursue their entrepreneurial aspirations with confidence.

Q.6. The Doctine of Indoor Management.

Ans. The doctrine of indoor management, also known as the Turquand rule, safeguards outsiders dealing with a company against internal irregularities. It allows individuals contracting with a company to presume that transactions are duly authorized by the company's articles and memorandum, without needing to scrutinize internal affairs. This principle, stemming from the Royal British Bank v Turquand case, holds companies liable for actions taken by their officers, even if internal procedures weren't followed. Exceptions include cases of forgery or when parties have knowledge or suspicion of irregularities. The doctrine ensures fairness for third parties while acknowledging the practical limitations of accessing internal company information.

Q.7. State the fact and legal principle established in the Ashbury Railway Carraige and Iron Co. Ltd. v Riche (1875) LR 7 HL 653.

Ans. **Fact:** In the case of Ashbury Railway Carriage and Iron Co Ltd v Riche (1875) LR 7 HL 653, the Ashbury Railway Carriage and Iron Company Ltd., incorporated under the Companies Act 1862, had a memorandum of association outlining its objects, including the manufacture and sale of railway carriages, as well as other activities such as purchasing and selling materials. Clause 4 of the memorandum specified that activities beyond those outlined in clause 3 required a special resolution.

Legal Principle Established: The House of Lords held that the contract entered into by the company to provide a loan for the construction of a railway in Belgium was ultra vires, meaning it was beyond the company's legal powers as defined in its memorandum of association. Consequently, the contract was deemed null and void and could not be ratified by the members of the company.

Significance: The Ashbury Railway Carriage and Iron Co Ltd v Riche case established the principle of ultra vires, which limited a company's activities to those explicitly permitted under its objects clause in the memorandum of association. This ruling highlighted the importance of adhering to the objects specified in the memorandum and provided clarity on the legal boundaries within which companies could operate.

Q.8. Difference between Public Company vs Private Company.

Ans. A company, an association formed for business activities, takes various forms under company laws, including Statutory Companies, Single Person Company, Companies Limited by shares, and more. Among these, Private and Public companies are prevalent.

Private Company:

A private company's shares aren't publicly available; they're held privately. Identified by "Private Limited (PVT LTD)" in its name, it enjoys the advantage of not needing to disclose financials to the public, being answerable only to its members/investors.

Public Company:

A public company, as per the Companies Act 2013, is listed on a stock exchange and can offer its securities to the general public through an Initial Public Offering (IPO). Shareholders can freely trade securities on stock exchanges, and the company must disclose its annual report to stakeholders.

Differences:

1. Listing: Public companies are listed on stock exchanges for public trading, while private companies aren't publicly traded.

2. Statutory Meeting: Not mandatory for private companies but is for public ones.

3. Minimum Members: Public companies require a minimum of seven members, while private companies need at least two.

4. Maximum Members: Public companies have no limit; private companies are capped at 200 members.

5. Directors:Public companies need at least three directors; private companies require a minimum of two.

6. AGM Quorum:Public companies require five members present; private companies need two.

7. Share Subscription: Public companies can invite the general public for share subscriptions; private companies cannot.

8. Prospectus:Mandatory for public companies, not for private ones.

9. Share Transfer: Public company shares can be freely transferred, while private company shares have restrictions.

10. Startup Requirements: Public companies need both a certificate of incorporation and commencement, while private companies only need a certificate of incorporation.

Public and private companies differ significantly in ownership structure, operational requirements, and regulatory obligations. Each type has its advantages and disadvantages, catering to different business needs and strategies.

Q.9. Discuss the Remedies against Oppression, Mismanagement and Prejudice as per Sections 241-246 of the 2013 Companies Act.

Ans. Sections 241-246 of the Companies Act of 2013 serve as a shield and remedy for company members, offering protection against acts of oppression, mismanagement, and prejudice by the majority or management that could detrimentally affect the company or public interest. These provisions empower the National Company Law Tribunal (NCLT) to intervene when necessary.

Oppression:

Actions detrimental to the public interest, the company's interests, or any member amount to oppression. However, oppression of a person in a role other than as a member may not be redressed under this provision. The foundational principles of oppression were established in S.P. Jain v. Kalinga Tubes Ltd., emphasizing burdensome, harsh, wrongful conduct lacking probity or fair dealing towards a member's proprietary rights. Subsequent cases further clarified that oppression requires more than just a lack of confidence between majority and minority shareholders; it necessitates continuous acts by majority shareholders. While a single act may suffice under certain circumstances, continuous acts are generally required to establish oppression.

Mismanagement:

Gross mismanagement detrimental to the company's interests or shareholders can be addressed under this provision. This includes actions such as diverting public money for unauthorized purposes or displaying gross negligence in managing affairs. However, mere unwise business decisions may not constitute mismanagement.

Prejudicial Acts:

The Companies Act of 2013 introduced protection against acts prejudicial to members' interests. While this concept hasn't been extensively interpreted, it generally refers to actions that unfairly disadvantage or harm petitioning shareholders. For example, issuing additional shares solely to alter shareholding patterns can be deemed prejudicial.

Just and Equitable Grounds for Winding Up:

Relief for oppression, mismanagement, or prejudice requires demonstrating that winding up the company is just and equitable but would unfairly prejudice the applicants. Grounds for winding up include loss of the company's business substratum or functional deadlock.

Numerical Threshold:

An action for oppression or mismanagement requires a minimum threshold of members holding at least 10% of the issued share capital or $1/10^{th}$ of total members, whichever is less. This threshold can be waived under exceptional circumstances.

Grant of Relief:

The NCLT has broad powers to redress grievances, including appointing administrators or committees to oversee the company's affairs. However, its authority is not absolute and does not extend to reinstating directors.

The Companies Act of 2013 safeguards minority shareholders' rights by providing avenues for relief against oppression, mismanagement, and prejudice. While stringent conditions must be met, these provisions ensure fairness and balance between minority and majority interests, promoting justice within corporate structures.

Q.10. State the powers and duties of Director as laid down in the Indian Companies Act.

Ans. Directors play a pivotal role in the governance and management of a company, acting as the custodians of its interests and ensuring its long-term success. The Companies Act of India, 2013 delineates the rights, duties, and liabilities of directors to ensure accountability, transparency, and ethical conduct within corporate structures. Let's break down these aspects:

Rights of Directors:

1. Authority to Exercise Powers: Directors have the authority, as per Section 291 of the Companies Act, to exercise all powers and perform actions on behalf of the company, subject to the provisions of the Act.

2. Formation of Committees: Directors can establish committees such as audit, nomination and remuneration, and stakeholder relationship committees to enhance corporate governance.

3. Appointment of Auditor: The board can select the company's first auditor within 30 days of incorporation, as per Section 224(6).

4. Contribution to Funds: Directors can contribute to charitable or political funds, subject to certain conditions outlined in Sections 181, 182, and 183.

5. Individual and Collective Rights: Directors have individual rights such as access to company records and notices of board meetings. Collectively, they have rights like refusing to transfer shares and electing a chairman.

Duties of Directors:

1. Compliance with Articles: Directors must act in accordance with the company's Articles of Association.

2. Fiduciary Duty:They are obligated to act in the best interests of the company and its stakeholders, exercising impartial judgment with due care, skill, and diligence.

3. Conflict of Interest: Directors must avoid conflicts of interest and disclose any potential conflicts to the board.

4. Authorization for Transactions: Certain transactions, like related-party transactions, require board approval to ensure they are in the company's best interests.

5. Confidentiality: Directors must maintain confidentiality of company information and trade secrets.

6. Liability for Violations: Directors can be held liable for breaches of duty, subject to fines and penalties outlined in the Act.

Liabilities of Directors:

1. Civil and Criminal Liability: Directors may face civil and criminal liabilities for actions that harm the company or violate regulatory requirements.

2. Tax Liability:Directors are liable for tax deficiencies unless they can prove non-negligence or violation of duty.

3. Derivative Actions: Shareholders can initiate derivative actions against directors for breaches of duty or fraud.

4. Insurance Coverage: Companies are required to purchase insurance to cover losses caused by directors, while directors can also purchase insurance for personal liability.

In conclusion, directors play a critical role in upholding corporate governance standards and safeguarding the interests of stakeholders. By adhering to their rights, fulfilling their duties, and mitigating liabilities, directors contribute to the overall success and sustainability of the company.

Q.11. What do you understand by the Memorandum of Association? Briefly state its various clauses and also write its difference from the Articles of Association.

Ans. The Memorandum of Association (MOA) is a crucial document for a company as it lays down the foundation and objectives upon which the company is incorporated. It defines the scope of a company's activities and its relationship with shareholders and stakeholders. Here are the key clauses typically found in a Memorandum of Association as per Section 4 of the Companies Act 2013:

1. Name Clause: It specifies the name of the company, which should end with the word "Limited" for a public limited company or "Private Limited" for a private limited company.

2. Registered Office Clause: This clause states the address of the registered office of the company, which is used for official communication and legal purposes.

3. Object Clause: The object clause outlines the main objectives and purposes for which the company is formed. It defines the scope of activities the company can engage in.

4. Liability Clause: It defines the liability of the company's members, which can be limited by shares or by guarantee, or unlimited.

5. Capital Clause: This clause states the amount of authorized share capital of the company and the division of shares into various classes.

On the other hand, the Articles of Association (AOA) contain rules and regulations for the internal management and administration of the company. Section 2(5) of the Companies Act 2013 defines the Articles of Association as a document that encapsulates the rules and regulations governing company affairs management. Here are some key differences between the Memorandum of Association and the Articles of Association:

1. Nature: The MOA defines the external relations and objectives of the company, while the AOA governs its internal management and conduct.

2. Amendment: The MOA can be altered, but only within the framework provided by the Companies Act, and with the approval of shareholders and regulatory authorities. The AOA can be amended by passing a special resolution at

a general meeting of the company.

3. Scope: The MOA defines the company's identity and its scope of activities, whereas the AOA deals with matters such as the rights and duties of shareholders, the appointment of directors, and the conduct of meetings.

To sum up, while the Memorandum of Association defines the company's external relations and objectives, the Articles of Association govern its internal management and conduct. Both documents are crucial for the formation and operation of a company under the Companies Act **2013**.

Q.12. What do you mean by Meeting? Discuss the kinds of meeting under the Companies Act, 2013.

Ans. While the Companies Act, 2013 doesn't explicitly define the term "meeting," in simple terms, a company meeting can be understood as the gathering of two or more individuals who come together, either by prior arrangement or unanimous agreement, to discuss and conduct legitimate business activities. Such meetings involve the assembly of members to deliberate and make decisions on important company matters. It can be considered as the convergence of a quorum of members to address both ordinary and special business affairs. Companies Act 2013, replacing its 1956 predecessor in India, provides detailed provisions regarding various types of meetings essential for company functioning. These gatherings serve as avenues for decision-making, communication, and transparency within organizational structures. This discourse will explore the diverse meeting types mandated by the Act and their significance in corporate governance.

Types of Meetings:

Board Meetings (Section 173):

Board meetings are pivotal for company management and administration. They must occur at least once every three months, with a minimum of four meetings annually. The quorum typically comprises one-third of total directors or two directors, whichever is higher. These sessions are critical for strategic decision-making and financial planning.

General Meetings (Section 96):

General meetings encompass shareholders' assemblies, including Annual General Meetings (AGMs) and Extraordinary General Meetings (EGMs). AGMs, held annually, discuss financial statements, appoint auditors, and approve dividends. EGMs address urgent matters necessitating immediate attention.

Annual General Meeting (Section 96):

The AGM stands as a paramount forum for shareholders, facilitating discussions on performance, financial statements, dividends, and director appointments. Typically, a minimum of 5 members must be present in person to constitute a quorum.

Extraordinary General Meeting (Section 100):

EGMs are convened for urgent matters such as changes in company constitution or share capital alterations. Notice periods are shorter than AGMs, and higher quorums are typically required.

Meeting of Creditors (Section 230):

Mandated during mergers, amalgamations, or reconstruction, these meetings enable creditors to voice opinions and vote on proposed agendas, impacting the company's future.

Meetings of Debenture Holders (Section 71):

Companies issuing debentures must convene meetings of debenture holders to discuss pertinent matters like interest rates and redemption.

General Provisions

Authority to Convene Meetings:

Meetings must be called by the board of directors, with resolutions adopted for such calls in compliance with the Companies Act 2013.

Notice:

Proper notices must be issued by the board, adhering to Act provisions, and sent to eligible members, detailing location, date, time, and meeting agenda.

Quorum:

Each meeting requires a minimum number of participants, ensuring decisions represent majority views.

Agenda:

Essential for structured discussions, agendas outline meeting topics, with deviations subject to member approval.

Minutes:

Accurate summaries of proceedings must be prepared and signed within 30 days of meeting conclusion.

Proxy:

Shareholders may appoint proxies to represent them at meetings.

Resolutions:

Transactions are formalized through resolutions, categorized as ordinary or special.

Conclusion

Meetings under the Companies Act 2013 are pivotal in India's corporate landscape, fostering transparency, accountability, and stakeholder engagement. Compliance with Act provisions regarding meetings not only fulfills legal obligations but also cultivates robust, ethical corporate environments. Companies prioritizing effective meetings enhance decision-making, navigate challenges adeptly, and foster stakeholder trust.

Q.13. Who are liable for mis-statement in the Prospectus? Discuss the extent of civil and criminal liability for such mis-statement.

Ans. Under the Companies Act 2013, liability for misstatements in a prospectus can extend to various parties involved in its preparation and dissemination. The extent of civil and criminal liability for such misstatements is delineated within the Act.

Liability for Misstatement in Prospectus:

Parties Liable:

1. Directors: Directors of the company are primarily responsible for the contents of the prospectus. They are expected to exercise due diligence in ensuring that all statements made therein are true and accurate.

2. Promoters: Promoters who have played a significant role in the formation of the company and in bringing it to the stage of issuing a prospectus can also be held liable for any misstatements.

3. Experts: Any expert whose opinion is included in the prospectus, such as auditors, accountants, or valuers, can also be held liable if their statements are found to be misleading or false.

4. Underwriters: Underwriters who have agreed to underwrite the issue of shares or debentures and have been named in the prospectus may also be held liable for misstatements.

Civil Liability (Section 34):

- Any person who has subscribed for securities offered on the basis of a prospectus containing a misstatement is entitled to compensation if they have suffered any loss as a result of relying on the misstatement. The liability is joint and several, meaning that any one or more of the parties mentioned above can be held liable.

Criminal Liability (Section 447):

- If a prospectus contains any statement that is false or misleading in any material particular or omits any material fact, the person responsible for the statement or the omission can be punished with imprisonment for a term which may extend to three years or with a fine which shall not be less than Rs. 50,000 but which may extend to Rs. 5,00,000, or with both.

Additional Provisions:

- Section 35 provides for civil liability for misstatements in reports, certificates, or other documents. Any person who authorizes the issue of such documents containing misstatements is liable to compensate any person who has suffered loss as a result.

- Section 36 imposes criminal liability for misstatements in reports, certificates, or other documents, similar to the provisions for prospectuses.

These provisions collectively aim to ensure the accuracy and reliability of information provided to potential investors and hold accountable those responsible for any misleading or false statements in prospectuses and related documents.

2018- Question Paper

Q.1. Annual General Meeting.

Ans. Oulined in section 96 of the Companies Act, the Annual General Meeting (AGM) is a mandatory annual gathering of shareholders and directors of a company, as per the Companies Act 2013. It serves as a vital platform for communication, decision-making, and accountability within the company. Here's an overview of the Annual General Meeting as per the Companies Act 2013:

Purpose:

1. Review Financial Statements: Shareholders review and approve the company's financial statements, including the balance sheet, profit and loss account, and cash flow statement.

2. Appointment of Auditors: Shareholders appoint or reappoint auditors for the upcoming financial year and fix their remuneration.

3. Declaration of Dividends: Shareholders decide on the declaration of dividends, if any, based on the company's profitability and financial performance.

4.*Appointment or Reappointment of Directors: Shareholders appoint or reappoint directors to the board, including independent directors, if applicable.

5. Any Other Business: Shareholders discuss and decide on any other matters brought before the meeting, including resolutions proposed by the board or shareholders.

Key Requirements:

1. Frequency: An AGM must be held by every company once every calendar year within six months from the end of the financial year.

2. Notice: A notice convening the AGM must be sent to all shareholders, directors, auditors, and other specified persons as per the Companies Act and Articles of Association. The notice period and contents are specified in the Act.

3. Quorum: The quorum for an AGM is typically a minimum number of shareholders present in person or through proxies to constitute a valid meeting. The quorum requirement is usually mentioned in the company's Articles of Association.

4. Chairperson: The chairperson of the board or, in their absence, another director appointed by the board presides over the AGM.

5. Recording Minutes: Detailed minutes of the AGM proceedings must be recorded and maintained by the company, including resolutions passed and voting results.

Special Business:

Any business considered special, such as alteration of the company's constitution, appointment of auditors, or approval of related party transactions, requires special resolutions passed by the shareholders at the AGM.

The Annual General Meeting is a crucial event in the corporate calendar, ensuring transparency, accountability, and shareholder participation in company affairs. Compliance with the Companies Act 2013 regarding AGMs is essential for maintaining good corporate governance practices and fostering trust among stakeholders.

Q.2. Who may be a member of a company?

Ans. Membership in a company is a fundamental concept, often used interchangeably with the term "shareholders." While typically every shareholder is considered a member and vice versa, there are exceptions to this rule. The process of becoming a member involves specific steps and criteria outlined by company law. Let's break down the concept of membership:

Introduction:

- The terms "members" and "shareholders" are commonly used interchangeably, though there are exceptions.

- A person may hold shares but not be considered a member until the transfer is officially registered in the company's books.

- Conversely, a member who has transferred shares remains a member until the transfer is formally registered.

Herdilia Unimers Ltd. v. Renu Jain:

- Shares' allotment, accompanied by the signing of share certificates and entry into the register of members, establishes membership, regardless of whether the shares are physically received.

Types of Members:

1. Company Limited by Shares: Shareholders are generally the members.

2. Company Limited by Guarantee: Individuals liable under the guarantee clause in the Memorandum of Association are members.

3. Unlimited Company: Individuals liable to contribute to the company's debts and liabilities upon winding-up are members.

Definition of Member (Section 2(55) of the Companies Act, 2013):

1.Subscribers to the Memorandum: Those who subscribe to the company's memorandum and are entered into the register of members upon registration.

2. Agreement in Writing: Any person who agrees in writing to become a member and is listed in the register of members becomes a member.

3. Beneficial Owners: Individuals holding shares listed as beneficial owners in depository records are deemed members.

Essential Elements:

- Agreement to Become a Member: The individual must agree to become a member.

- Entry in Register of Members: The person's name must be entered into the company's register of members.

Balkrishan Gupta v. Swadeshi Polytex Ltd.:

- Two crucial elements for membership are the agreement to become a member and the registration of the individual's name in the company's register of members.

Understanding membership in a company involves recognizing the legal requirements and processes that govern the relationship between shareholders and the company.

Q.3. Types of Comapnies.

Ans. Let's explore the important types of companies:

Classification by Mode of Incorporation:

A. Chartered Companies:

- Chartered companies are established under a special charter by a monarch. Examples include The East India Company and The Bank of England in England.

- Their powers and business nature are defined by the charter, granting them broad authority.

- The Sovereign can annul the charter and dissolve the company if it deviates from the prescribed business.

- Not common in India.

B. Statutory Companies:

- These companies are incorporated by a Special Act passed by the Central or State legislature.

- Examples include the Reserve Bank of India, State Bank of India, and Life Insurance Corporation.

- They derive their powers from the Acts constituting them and have no memorandum or articles of association.

- Legislative amendments can alter their powers.

C. Registered or Incorporated Companies:

- Formed under the Companies Act, 1956, or earlier Company Acts.

- Come into existence upon registration under the Act and issuance of a certificate of incorporation by the Registrar of Companies.

- Further divided into:

i) Companies Limited by Shares: Shareholders' liability is limited to the face value of their subscribed shares. They can be public or private companies.

ii) Companies Limited by Guarantee: Members promise to pay a fixed sum in the event of liquidation. Common in non-profit sectors.

iii) Unlimited Companies: Members have unlimited liability. They can be public or private companies.

On the Basis of Number of Members:

1. Private Company:

- Limited to a maximum of fifty members, excluding certain categories as per Sec. 3(1)(iii) of the Indian Companies Act, 1956.

- Restricts the right to transfer shares, limits the number of members, and prohibits public subscription.

- Requires a minimum of two members to form, and the name must include "Pvt" at the end.

2. Public Company:

- Any company that is not a private company.

- Does not restrict share transfer, imposes no maximum member limit, and invites the public to subscribe to its shares and debentures.

Differences between Public and Private Companies:

1. Minimum number of members: 7 for public, 2 for private.

2. Maximum number of members: No restriction for public, max 50 for private.

3. Number of directors: Minimum 3 for public, 2 for private.

4. Invitation for share subscription: Public companies invite the public, private companies do not.

5. Name: Private companies include "Private Limited" in their name.

6. Public subscription: Only public companies can invite the public to purchase shares.

7. Issue of prospectus: Private companies are not required to issue a prospectus.

8. Transferability of shares: Shares in public companies are freely transferable.

9. Special privileges: Private companies enjoy some special privileges not available to public companies.

10. Quorum: Different quorum requirements for meetings.

11. Managerial remuneration: Restrictions on total managerial remuneration for public companies.

12. Commencement of business: Public companies need a "Certificate of Commencement of Business" before starting operations.

Q.4. write a short note on Dividend

Ans. Dividends are distributions of a company's profits to its shareholders. They serve as a reward for investing in the company and represent a portion of its earnings. Dividends can be issued regularly, typically quarterly, or as one-time payments. They provide investors with a steady income stream and are often a key factor in determining the attractiveness of a stock. Companies may opt to reinvest profits instead of distributing dividends to fuel growth or maintain liquidity. Dividend payments are influenced by factors such as profitability, cash flow, and management's dividend policy, impacting shareholder returns and investor confidence.

Q.5. Reduction of Share Capital

Ans. Reduction of share capital refers to the process by which a company decreases the total amount of its issued share capital. This can be done for various reasons, including restructuring, financial reorganization, or returning surplus capital to shareholders. The reduction typically involves cancelling or repurchasing existing shares, thereby reducing the company's equity base. Shareholders may benefit from increased earnings per share and improved financial ratios following the reduction. However, this process is subject to regulatory scrutiny and often requires approval from shareholders and relevant authorities to ensure protection of creditors' interests and compliance with legal requirements.

Q.6. What is the difference between a shareholder and a debenture holder? Explain.

Ans. A shareholder is an owner of a company who holds equity in the business through ownership of shares. Shareholders have ownership rights, such as voting rights and the right to receive dividends, and they bear the risk of the company's performance.

On the other hand, a debenture holder is a creditor of the company who lends money to the company by purchasing debentures. Debenture holders do not have ownership rights but are entitled to receive fixed interest payments and repayment of principal amount as per the terms of the debenture agreement. They are considered creditors and have priority over shareholders in case of liquidation, as they are owed money before shareholders receive any distribution.

Q.7. What do you mean by the doctrine of Indoor Managment

Ans. The doctrine of Indoor Management, also known as the Turquand Rule, is a legal principle that protects third parties dealing with a company from the consequences of the company's internal irregularities. It states that outsiders are entitled to assume that internal company procedures have been properly followed, even if they are not aware of the company's internal rules. This doctrine acts as a safeguard for innocent parties who rely on the apparent authority of officers or agents of the company in their dealings, shielding them from liability if the company's internal management has not adhered to its own rules.

Q.8. 'Prospectus must state truth and nothing but truth.' Do you agree with the statement?

Ans. The statement "Prospectus must state truth and nothing but truth" encapsulates a fundamental principle in securities regulation and investor protection. Transparency and accuracy in the information provided in a prospectus are paramount to ensure investors can make informed decisions. Misrepresentation or omission of material facts can distort investors' perceptions of the risks and rewards associated with an investment, leading to potential financial losses and undermining market integrity.

It's crucial for prospectuses to adhere strictly to truthfulness and accuracy standards. Any deviation from this principle not only violates legal and ethical obligations but also erodes trust in the financial markets. Investors rely on prospectuses as primary sources of information when evaluating investment opportunities, and any falsehoods can lead to legal liabilities for the issuing company and its directors.

In essence, the integrity of the financial system hinges on the adherence to this principle, safeguarding the interests of investors and upholding the credibility of capital markets.

Q.9. State the circumstances under which the corportate veil of a company is lifted and separate legal existence of it is ignored.

Ans. The corporate veil, which separates the legal identity of a company from its shareholders, directors, and officers, can be lifted or pierced under certain circumstances. These circumstances typically involve situations where the company's separate legal personality is abused or misused to perpetrate fraud, injustice, or wrongdoing. Here are common scenarios where the corporate veil may be pierced:

Fraudulent or Improper Conduct: When the corporate structure is used to conceal fraudulent activities or to perpetrate a fraud on creditors, shareholders, or other stakeholders, courts may lift the corporate veil to hold responsible individuals accountable.

Sham Companies: If a company is established as a mere facade to disguise the true intentions of its controllers or to evade legal obligations, courts may disregard its separate legal existence and hold the controllers personally liable for the company's actions.

Agency or Alter Ego: When the company and its controllers operate as alter egos or agents of each other, blurring the distinction between personal and corporate affairs, courts may pierce the corporate veil to prevent injustice or unfairness.

Group of Companies: In cases involving a group of companies, where one company dominates or controls another to the extent that they are effectively operating as a single entity, courts may disregard the separate legal identities and hold the group collectively liable.

Public Interest: In exceptional circumstances involving matters of public interest or where adherence to corporate formalities would defeat the purpose of the law, courts may lift the corporate veil to achieve justice and equity.

In each of these situations, courts carefully assess the specific facts and circumstances to determine whether piercing the corporate veil is warranted to prevent abuse and ensure fairness in legal proceedings.

Q.10. How directors of a company can be appointed? Discuss the provisions relating to the removal of the directors.

Ans. Directors of a company can be appointed through various means as per the company's articles of association and relevant laws. Common methods of director appointment include:

Appointment by Shareholders: Shareholders can appoint directors through a resolution passed at a general meeting. Nomination and election processes are typically outlined in the company's articles of association.

Appointment by Board: Existing directors or the board of directors themselves may have the authority to appoint additional directors to fill vacancies or to meet specific requirements. However, such appointments may be subject to approval by shareholders at the next general meeting.

Appointment by Third Parties: In certain cases, such as when a company receives investment from venture capitalists or private equity firms, these external parties may have the right to appoint directors to represent their interests.

Regarding the removal of directors, provisions are typically outlined in the company's articles of association and relevant laws. Directors can usually be removed by:

Shareholder Resolution: Shareholders can pass a resolution at a general meeting to remove a director before the expiration of their term. Depending on the jurisdiction and the company's articles, a special majority or simple majority may be required.

Board Resolution: In some cases, the board of directors may have the authority to remove a director, subject to compliance with legal requirements and the company's articles.

Court Order: In exceptional circumstances, such as instances of director misconduct or breach of fiduciary duties, shareholders or regulatory authorities may seek court intervention to remove a director. The court may issue an order for removal if it deems it necessary to protect the interests of the company and its stakeholders.

The appointment and removal of directors are governed by legal provisions, the company's articles of association, and principles of corporate governance aimed at ensuring effective leadership and accountability within the company.

Q.11. What do you understand by the rule of majority. Discuss the circumstances when this rule is discarded for protective minority of share holders. Refer to case law.

Ans. The rule of majority in corporate governance refers to the principle that decisions made by a majority of shareholders or directors are binding on the company and all its stakeholders. This rule ensures efficient decision-making and promotes the interests of the majority of shareholders. However, there are circumstances where the rule of majority may be discarded in favor of protecting the rights of minority shareholders.

One such circumstance is when the majority exercises its power in a manner that unfairly prejudices the interests of minority shareholders. In such cases, courts may intervene to safeguard the rights of minority shareholders and prevent oppressive or unfair conduct by the majority. This principle is often referred to as the principle of protective minority.

A landmark case illustrating the application of the protective minority principle is Foss v. Harbottle (1843) where the court held that minority shareholders have the right to bring a derivative action on behalf of the company if the majority acts unlawfully or oppressively. Similarly, in Re Saul D. Harrison & Sons plc (1995), the court held that a scheme of arrangement unfairly prejudiced minority shareholders and intervened to protect their interests.

These cases underscore the importance of balancing the rights of majority shareholders with the need to protect minority shareholders from oppressive or unfair actions, even if it means disregarding the rule of majority in certain circumstances.

Q.12. When Court can order winding up of a Company on just and equitable grounds?

Ans. A court can order the winding up of a company on "just and equitable" grounds when it deems that it's necessary to dissolve the company for reasons of fairness and justice. This provision is typically invoked when there's a breakdown in the relationship between shareholders or directors, and continuing the company's operations would be prejudicial to the interests of one or more shareholders.

Just and equitable grounds can include a variety of circumstances such as:

Oppression of Minority Shareholders: If majority shareholders are unfairly treating minority shareholders, such as by excluding them from decision-making processes or misusing company funds.

Deadlock: When there's a deadlock in decision-making between shareholders or directors that prevents the company from functioning effectively.

Fraud or Mismanagement: Instances where there's evidence of fraud, mismanagement, or illegal activities within the company, jeopardizing the interests of shareholders.

Ultra Vires Acts: If the company engages in acts beyond its legal authority, violating its constitution or the law.

Loss of Substratum: When the company's original purpose or business has become impossible to achieve or has ceased to exist.

The court may order the winding up of the company to protect the interests of the aggrieved parties or to prevent further harm. Winding up provides a legal mechanism for the orderly dissolution of the company and the distribution of its assets among creditors and shareholders according to established priorities.

Q.13. Distinguish between Memorandum of Association and Articles of Association. Explain their Contents.

Ans. In accordance with The Companies Act 2013, the Memorandum of Association (MOA) and Articles of Association (AOA) are two vital documents governing the formation and operation of a company in India. Here's how they differ and what each document contains:

1. Memorandum of Association (MOA):

- Purpose: The MOA outlines the fundamental objectives and scope of activities that a company intends to undertake upon its incorporation.

- Contents:

- Name Clause: Specifies the name of the company, which should end with the word "Limited" in the case of a public company or "Private Limited" in the case of a private company.

- Registered Office Clause: States the official address of the company.

- Object Clause: Enumerates the main objectives for which the company is established. These objectives define the scope of the company's activities and serve as a guideline for its operations.

- Liability Clause: Specifies the liability of members of the company, which can be limited by shares or guarantee or be unlimited.

- Capital Clause: Details the authorized capital of the company and the division of share capital into shares, including the nominal value of each share.

- Association Clause: Contains a declaration signed by the subscribers (initial shareholders) expressing their intention to form a company and become members.

2. Articles of Association (AOA):

- Purpose: The AOA lays down the rules and regulations for the internal management and administration of the company, as well as the rights and duties of its members and directors.

- Contents:

- Preliminary Clause: Specifies that the regulations contained in the AOA are adopted by the company's shareholders and will govern its internal affairs.

- Definitions Clause: Clarifies the meanings of key terms used throughout the AOA.

- Shares and Share Capital Clause: Details the rights and obligations of shareholders, including the issuance and transfer of shares, share certificates, and dividends.

- Management and Administration Clause: Sets out the powers and duties of the board of directors, including the appointment, removal, and powers of directors, as well as procedures for board meetings.

- Borrowing Powers Clause: Specifies the limits and procedures for borrowing money by the company.

-Dividends and Reserves Clause: Outlines the rules governing the declaration and payment of dividends, as well as the creation of reserves.

-Winding-Up Clause: Provides procedures for the dissolution and winding-up of the company, including the distribution of assets among shareholders.

- Miscellaneous Clause: Covers any other provisions deemed necessary for the internal management and administration of the company.

To conclude, while the Memorandum of Association defines the company's external objectives and scope of activities, the Articles of Association establish the internal rules and regulations governing its operation and management. Together, these documents form the constitutional framework of a company and provide guidance for its stakeholders.

2017 -Question Paper

Q.1. Doctrine of constructive notice.

Ans. The doctrine of constructive notice, as outlined in The Companies Act 2013, refers to a legal principle that imputes knowledge of certain information to all persons dealing with a company. Under this doctrine, any person entering into a transaction with a company is deemed to have constructive notice of the company's constitutional documents, including its Memorandum of Association (MOA) and Articles of Association (AOA), as well as any other publicly available documents filed with the Registrar of Companies.

Key points regarding the doctrine of constructive notice under The Companies Act 2013 include:

1. Public Inspection: The MOA and AOA of a company, along with other statutory documents such as annual returns, financial statements, and resolutions passed by the company, are required to be filed with the Registrar of Companies. These documents are available for public inspection, either physically at the Registrar's office or through online portals.

2. Presumption of Knowledge: Any person dealing with a company, whether as a shareholder, creditor, or other third party, is presumed to have knowledge of the company's constitutional documents and other relevant information contained in public records. This presumption arises irrespective of whether the person has actually examined the documents.

3.Reliance on Public Records: Courts may impute constructive notice to parties who fail to conduct reasonable inquiries or investigations into the company's affairs before entering into transactions with it. This implies that parties are expected to rely on the information available in public records and to take it into consideration when dealing with the company.

4. Protection of Third Parties: The doctrine of constructive notice serves to protect the interests of third parties who transact with companies by ensuring that they are aware of the company's legal obligations, powers, and limitations as set out in its constitutional documents. It promotes transparency and accountability in corporate dealings.

5.Legal Consequences: Failure to comply with the requirements of the doctrine of constructive notice may have legal consequences. For example, a person who enters into a transaction with a company cannot later claim ignorance of the company's constitutional provisions as a defense in legal proceedings arising from the transaction.

To sum up, the doctrine of constructive notice under The Companies Act 2013 operates to impute knowledge of a company's constitutional documents and other relevant information to all persons dealing with the company, thereby promoting transparency, accountability, and legal certainty in corporate transactions.

Q.2. Rule of Majority.

Ans. The rule of majority, as enshrined in The Companies Act 2013, is a fundamental principle governing the decision-making process within a company. It stipulates that decisions made by a majority of shareholders or directors during a validly convened meeting are binding on the company and all its members. The Companies Act 2013 contains provisions outlining the rule of majority in various sections, primarily concerning meetings of shareholders and directors. Here's how the rule of majority is reflected in the Act:

1. Section 103: Ordinary and Special Resolutions:

- This section distinguishes between ordinary and special resolutions, with certain matters requiring approval by a higher threshold of votes.

- Ordinary resolutions typically require a simple majority of votes cast by shareholders present in person or by proxy at a general meeting.

- Special resolutions, on the other hand, require a higher majority, usually three-fourths or more of the votes cast by shareholders entitled to vote.

2. Section 110: Postal Ballot:

- Section 110 of the Act allows companies to conduct certain business through a postal ballot, enabling shareholders to vote on resolutions without attending a physical meeting.

- Resolutions passed through a postal ballot must adhere to the same requirements for ordinary or special resolutions, depending on the nature of the business.

3. Section 173: Meetings of Board:

- This section governs the meetings of the board of directors of a company.
- Decisions of the board are generally made by a majority of directors present at a meeting, with each director having one vote.
- The Act allows directors to participate in meetings through electronic means, provided all directors can hear and participate in the proceedings.

4. Section 174: Quorum for Meetings:

- Section 174 specifies the minimum number of directors required to be present for a board meeting to be valid.
- The quorum for board meetings is typically one-third of the total number of directors or a higher number as prescribed in the company's articles of association.

5. Section 186: Restrictions on Powers of Board:

- Section 186 imposes certain restrictions on the powers of the board of directors, requiring specific matters to be approved by shareholders through ordinary or special resolutions.
- For instance, transactions involving the sale, lease, or disposal of the company's undertaking require approval by an ordinary resolution passed by shareholders.

6. Section 196: Appointment of Managing Director, Whole-time Director, or Manager:

- This section mandates that the appointment, reappointment, or variation of the terms of appointment of a managing director, whole-time director, or manager must be approved by shareholders through an ordinary resolution.

Overall, the rule of majority under The Companies Act 2013 ensures that decisions affecting the company's governance and operations are made in accordance with the will of the majority of shareholders or directors, thereby safeguarding the interests of the company and its stakeholders.

Q.3. Share Capital.

Ans.

Under The Companies Act 2013, the concept of share capital is regulated by several sections. Here's an overview of the relevant sections pertaining to share capital:

1. Section 61: Power to Alter Share Capital:

- This section empowers a company to alter its share capital subject to the provisions of its memorandum and articles of association.
- Alteration of share capital can be achieved through various means, such as increasing, reducing, consolidating, dividing, or converting shares.

2. Section 62: Further Issue of Share Capital:

- Section 62 deals with the issuance of further shares, whether by way of a rights issue, preferential allotment, private placement, or bonus issue.
- It outlines the procedures and conditions that must be followed for the issuance of new shares, including obtaining approval from shareholders and complying with regulatory requirements.

3. Section 63: Issue of Bonus Shares:

- This section pertains specifically to the issue of bonus shares by a company.
- It allows a company to capitalize its reserves and surplus to issue bonus shares to existing shareholders without requiring them to pay any additional consideration.

4. Section 64: Notice to Registrar for Alteration of Share Capital:

- Section 64 mandates that a company must give notice to the Registrar of Companies regarding any alteration of its share capital.
- The notice must be accompanied by a resolution authorizing the alteration and a copy of the altered memorandum of association.

5. Section 65: Unlimited Company to Provide for Reserve Share Capital on Conversion into a Limited Company**:

- This section applies when an unlimited company decides to convert into a limited company.

- It requires the company to provide for a reserve share capital upon conversion, which serves as a protection for creditors.

6. Section 66: Reduction of Share Capital:

- Section 66 deals with the reduction of share capital by a company.

- It outlines the procedures and requirements for reducing share capital, including obtaining approval from shareholders, creditors, and the National Company Law Tribunal (NCLT).

7. Section 67: Restrictions on Purchase by Company or Giving of Loans by it for Purchase of Its Shares**:

- This section imposes restrictions on a company's ability to purchase its own shares or provide loans for the purchase of its shares.

- It aims to prevent companies from using their funds to manipulate their share prices or unduly influence their share capital structure.

These sections collectively govern various aspects of share capital, including its alteration, issuance, reduction, and related matters, ensuring transparency, accountability, and compliance with legal requirements in corporate transactions.

Q.4. Annual General Meeting.

Ans. Under The Companies Act 2013, an Annual General Meeting (AGM) is defined in Sections 96 and 97. Here's how it is defined and regulated:

1. Section 96: Annual General Meeting:

- According to Section 96 of The Companies Act 2013, every company is required to convene an AGM every year.

- The AGM must be held within six months from the end of the financial year of the company.

- The purpose of the AGM is to transact the following business:

- Consideration and adoption of the financial statements (including the balance sheet, profit and loss account, and any other documents required to be attached thereto).

- Declaration of dividend, if any.

- Appointment or reappointment of directors and auditors.

- Ratification of the appointment of auditors.

- Any other business as may be specified in the notice convening the meeting or as permitted by the Chairman.

2. Section 97: Power of Tribunal to call Annual General Meeting:

- Section 97 of the Act empowers the National Company Law Tribunal (NCLT) to call or direct the calling of an AGM if the default is made in holding the AGM or the AGM cannot be held.

- The NCLT may do so either on its own motion or on the application of any director or member of the company who would be entitled to vote at the meeting.

Let us conclude that an AGM under The Companies Act 2013 is a mandatory annual meeting convened by every company within six months from the end of its financial year. The AGM serves as a platform for shareholders to discuss and transact various matters related to the company's financial performance, governance, and appointment of key personnel, among other things. Failure to hold an AGM or comply with its requirements may result in regulatory action by the NCLT.

Q.5. Modes of winding up of a company.

Ans. Under The Companies Act 2013, there are primarily three modes of winding up a company: voluntary winding up, winding up by the Tribunal (court), and winding up subject to supervision of the Tribunal. Here's an overview of each mode along with landmark case law associated with winding up:

1. Voluntary Winding Up (Sections 59-61):

- Definition: Voluntary winding up occurs when the members or creditors of a company resolve to wind up the affairs of the company voluntarily.

- Procedure: The process of voluntary winding up involves passing a special resolution by the members or creditors, appointing a liquidator, settling the company's debts, and distributing its assets among the stakeholders.

- Case Law: Re Noon Products Ltd* [1961] Ch 24: This landmark case established the principle that a resolution for voluntary winding up must be passed by a simple majority of members in a general meeting and must be confirmed by a subsequent resolution passed by a three-fourth majority.

2. Winding Up by the Tribunal (Sections 272-303):
- Definition: Winding up by the Tribunal (court) occurs when the Tribunal, upon petition by the company, creditors, or any other interested party, orders the compulsory winding up of the company.
- Procedure: The process involves filing a winding-up petition with the Tribunal, which may be based on grounds such as the company's inability to pay its debts, just and equitable grounds, or failure to commence business within a year of incorporation.
- Case Law: In Re Hind Overseas Pvt. Ltd.* (2013) 177 CompCas 142 (Del): This case established the principle that winding up on just and equitable grounds can be ordered by the Tribunal if the court is satisfied that the company's affairs are being conducted in a manner prejudicial to the interests of its members or in a manner oppressive to some part of the members.
   3. Winding Up Subject to Supervision of the Tribunal (Section 275):
- Definition: Winding up subject to the supervision of the Tribunal is a hybrid mode of winding up where the company liquidates its assets and distributes them among the creditors under the supervision of the Tribunal.
- Procedure: The company or creditors initiate the process by filing a petition for winding up subject to the supervision of the Tribunal, and once the order is passed, the liquidation process is conducted under the Tribunal's oversight.
- Case Law: Swastik Industries Ltd. v. State of Gujarat* (2021) SCC Online Guj 2945: This case highlighted the importance of judicial supervision in winding up subject to the supervision of the Tribunal to ensure fair and equitable distribution of the company's assets among creditors.

These modes of winding up provide legal mechanisms for the orderly dissolution of companies and the distribution of their assets among stakeholders in accordance with the provisions of The Companies Act 2013. Landmark case law further elucidates the principles and procedures governing each mode of winding up, ensuring clarity and consistency in judicial interpretation and application.

Q.6. What do you understand by "Memorandum of Association" of a company?

Ans. Under The Companies Act 2013, the Memorandum of Association (MOA) of a company is defined under Section 4. It serves as the charter or constitution of the company, outlining its fundamental objectives, scope of activities, and powers. The MOA specifies the company's name, registered office, objects clause, liability clause, and capital clause. Any act undertaken by a company beyond the scope of its MOA is considered ultra vires (beyond the powers) and therefore void.

Section 4 of The Companies Act 2013 states:

"4. (1) The memorandum of a company shall state—

(a) the name of the company;

(b) the state in which the registered office of the company is to be situated;

(c) the objects for which the company is incorporated and any matter considered necessary in furtherance thereof;

(d) the liability of members of the company—

(i) in the case of a company limited by shares, the amount of share capital they have undertaken to contribute; and

(ii) in the case of a company limited by guarantee, the amount up to which they have undertaken to contribute in the event of its being wound up;

(e) in the case of a company having a share capital—

(i) the amount of share capital with which the company is to be registered and its division into shares of a fixed amount;

(ii) the number of shares taken and the amount paid on each share; and

(iii) the names of the subscribers to the memorandum and the number of shares subscribed by them, respectively, and their written consent to take the shares."

Landmark case law related to the Memorandum of Association includes:

1. Ashbury Railway Carriage and Iron Co. Ltd. v. Riche (1875): This case established the principle that a company's powers are limited to those expressly stated in its MOA, along with any necessary implications. Any act performed by the company beyond these powers would be ultra vires and void.

2. In Re Jon Beauforte (London) Ltd. (1953): This case reaffirmed the principle of ultra vires and held that any transaction undertaken by a company outside the scope of its MOA is void, even if it was for the company's benefit.

These cases highlight the importance of the MOA as the foundational document governing a company's activities and the legal consequences of acting beyond its prescribed powers.

Q.7. Discuss different kinds of shares.

Ans. Under The Companies Act 2013, shares represent ownership interests in a company and are classified into different categories based on their rights, obligations, and characteristics. Here are the various kinds of shares defined under sections of the Act, along with a landmark case law relevant to each type:

1. Equity Shares:

- Definition: Equity shares represent the ordinary share capital of a company and typically carry voting rights, dividends, and residual claim on the company's assets.

- Case Law: In the landmark case of Foss v. Harbottle (1843), it was established that the shareholders collectively own the company's assets and can enforce their rights through majority decisions in general meetings, thus protecting the principle of majority rule.

2. Preference Shares:

- Definition: Preference shares are shares that carry preferential rights over equity shares with regard to dividend payments and repayment of capital in the event of liquidation. They may be cumulative or non-cumulative.

- Case Law: In Hind Overseas Pvt. Ltd. v. Raghunath Prasad Jhunjhunwala (1976), the Supreme Court of India held that preference shareholders are entitled to enforce their rights independently of the company's management and are entitled to payment of dividends as per the terms of the preference share issue.

3. Cumulative Preference Shares:

- Definition: Cumulative preference shares entitle shareholders to accumulate unpaid dividends if the company is unable to pay dividends in any particular year.

- Case Law: The case of Gramophone and Typewriter Ltd. v. Stanley (1908) established that cumulative preference shareholders have the right to receive arrears of dividend before equity shareholders are entitled to any dividend payment.

4. Non-cumulative Preference Shares:

- Definition: Non-cumulative preference shares do not allow the accumulation of unpaid dividends. If dividends are not paid in any year, the right to receive them lapses.

- Case Law: While there isn't a specific landmark case for non-cumulative preference shares, the rights and obligations of shareholders in this category are typically determined by the terms of the share issue and the company's articles of association.

5. Redeemable Preference Shares:

- Definition: Redeemable preference shares are shares that can be redeemed by the company after a specified period or at the company's discretion, subject to compliance with legal requirements.

- Case Law: In Berman v. Alperovich (1917), the court held that redeemable preference shares are akin to a debt owing from the company to the shareholder, and therefore, the company must comply with the terms of redemption specified at the time of issue.

6. Convertible Preference Shares:

- Definition: Convertible preference shares are preference shares that can be converted into equity shares after a certain period or under specified conditions.

- Case Law: The case of Haji Abdulla Haji Adam v. Balkrishna Ramchandra Nayan (1938) affirmed the principle that the terms of conversion of preference shares into equity shares must be clearly stated in the company's articles of association and complied with by both the company and the shareholders.

These different kinds of shares provide companies with flexibility in structuring their capital and offering varied rights and benefits to different classes of shareholders. Landmark cases have played a crucial role in defining the rights and obligations associated with each type of share, ensuring clarity and legal certainty in corporate transactions.

Q.8. Discuss briefly the powers, functions and position of director in a company.

Ans. Under The Companies Act 2013, directors play a pivotal role in the management and administration of a company. Here's a brief overview of their powers, functions, and position, along with relevant sections of the Act and a landmark case law:

1. Powers of Directors:

- Section 179 of The Companies Act 2013 enumerates the powers of directors, which include the authority to make decisions related to the day-to-day operations of the company, enter into contracts, appoint officers, and represent the company in legal proceedings, among others.

- Directors are vested with the power to act collectively through board meetings and resolutions, as well as individually when duly authorized by the board.

2. Functions of Directors:

- Directors are responsible for overseeing the management and affairs of the company, ensuring compliance with statutory requirements, and safeguarding the interests of shareholders.

- They are tasked with making strategic decisions, setting company objectives, and formulating policies to achieve corporate goals.

- Directors also have a fiduciary duty to act in the best interests of the company and exercise due diligence, care, and skill in their decision-making processes.

3. Position of Directors:

- Directors hold a position of trust and confidence within the company and owe fiduciary duties to shareholders, employees, creditors, and other stakeholders.

- They are appointed by shareholders and may be classified as executive or non-executive directors based on their involvement in the day-to-day management of the company.

- The board of directors collectively constitutes the highest decision-making authority in the company, with directors serving as its members.

Landmark Case Law: One of the seminal cases in corporate law concerning the duties and liabilities of directors is *Foss v. Harbottle* (1843). In this case, the court established the principle of corporate personality and held that only the company, not individual shareholders, has the standing to bring a claim for damages caused by directors' actions. This ruling underscored the distinction between the company as a separate legal entity and its members, highlighting the limited recourse available to shareholders in cases of corporate mismanagement.

Furthermore, *Salomon v. Salomon & Co. Ltd.* (1897) is another landmark case that affirmed the separate legal personality of a company from its shareholders. In this case, the House of Lords held that a company is a distinct legal entity capable of entering into contracts and suing or being sued in its own name. This decision established the foundational principle of corporate law and reinforced the concept of limited liability, providing protection to shareholders from personal liability for the company's debts.

These landmark cases underscore the importance of directors' duties and the legal framework governing their actions, highlighting the need for directors to act in the best interests of the company while upholding their fiduciary duties to stakeholders.

Q.9. Explain the statutory requirements for the registration of a company and also discuss the advantages and disadvantages of incorporation of a company.

Ans. The statutory requirements for the registration of a company under The Companies Act 2013 encompass several key steps and provisions outlined in the legislation. Additionally, the advantages and disadvantages of incorporating a company are also delineated within the Act, supported by landmark case law. Let's break down each aspect:

Statutory Requirements for Company Registration:

1. Name Reservation: The first step is to reserve a unique name for the proposed company, complying with the guidelines laid down by the Registrar of Companies (RoC).

2. Memorandum of Association (MOA) and Articles of Association (AOA): Draft and file the MOA and AOA, which contain details regarding the company's objectives, capital structure, internal management rules, and other relevant provisions.

3. Director Identification Number (DIN): Obtain a DIN for all proposed directors of the company. DIN is a unique identification number required for appointment as a director.

4. Digital Signature Certificate (DSC): Acquire DSCs for all proposed directors. DSCs are necessary for filing electronic documents with the RoC.

5. Registered Office: Furnish details of the registered office address of the company, which must be filed with the RoC.

6. Payment of Fees and Stamp Duty: Pay the requisite fees and stamp duty for the incorporation of the company.

7. Filing of Incorporation Documents: Submit all necessary documents, including the MOA, AOA, identity proof, address proof, and other prescribed forms, to the RoC for incorporation.

8. Certificate of Incorporation: Upon approval of the application, the RoC issues a Certificate of Incorporation, signifying the legal existence of the company.

Advantages and Disadvantages of Incorporation:

Advantages:

1. Limited Liability: Shareholders enjoy limited liability, restricting their personal liability to the extent of their investment in the company. This protects personal assets from business liabilities.

2. Separate Legal Entity: A company has a distinct legal personality separate from its shareholders, allowing it to enter into contracts, sue, and be sued in its own name.

3. Access to Capital: Companies can raise capital by issuing shares to the public or private investors, facilitating growth and expansion opportunities.

4. Perpetual Succession: A company enjoys perpetual succession, meaning its existence is unaffected by changes in its membership, ensuring continuity in operations.

5. Tax Benefits: Companies may be eligible for certain tax benefits, such as deductions for business expenses and favorable tax rates on corporate profits.

Disadvantages:

1. Compliance Burden: Companies are subject to extensive regulatory compliance requirements, including periodic filings, board meetings, and financial disclosures, which may entail administrative burdens and costs.

2. Complex Formation Process: The process of incorporating a company involves various legal formalities, documentation, and procedural requirements, potentially leading to delays and complexities.

3. Public Scrutiny: Public companies are subject to greater public scrutiny and disclosure obligations, which may restrict confidentiality and privacy.

4. Costs: Establishing and maintaining a company entails costs, including registration fees, legal fees, and ongoing operational expenses, which may be significant, especially for small businesses.

Landmark Case Law:

One notable case demonstrating the significance of incorporation and limited liability is Salomon v Salomon & Co Ltd (1897). In this case, the House of Lords affirmed the principle of separate legal personality, ruling that a company is distinct from its shareholders. Mr. Salomon, the sole shareholder of a company, sought to limit his liability by incorporating the business. When the company later faced insolvency, creditors attempted to hold Mr. Salomon personally liable for the company's debts. However, the court upheld the company's separate legal identity, shielding Mr. Salomon from personal liability beyond his investment in the company. This case established a cornerstone principle of company law, emphasizing the importance of incorporation for limiting personal liability and protecting shareholders' interests.

Thus, The Companies Act 2013 lays down comprehensive provisions for the registration of companies, while also delineating the advantages and disadvantages of incorporation. Landmark case law, such as Salomon v Salomon & Co

Ltd, reinforces the legal principles underlying corporate structure and limited liability.

Q.10. What is doctrine of 'Indoor Management'? Discuss with the help of decided cases.

Ans. The doctrine of "Indoor Management," also known as the "Turquand Rule" or "Rule in Royal British Bank v Turquand," is a legal principle that provides protection to outsiders who enter into transactions with a company on the assumption that the company's internal procedures have been duly followed. This doctrine operates as a counterpart to the doctrine of constructive notice and aims to balance the interests of third parties dealing with a company by protecting them against the internal irregularities of the company's management.

Under the doctrine of Indoor Management, third parties are entitled to assume that internal company procedures have been properly followed, even if this may not be the case. This assumption is based on the rationale that outsiders cannot be expected to have knowledge of the company's internal affairs, unlike the public documents available for inspection under the doctrine of constructive notice.

Key provisions of The Companies Act 2013 relevant to the doctrine of Indoor Management include Section 128, which deals with the registration of charges, and Section 139, which pertains to the validity of acts of directors and other officers.

The landmark case that established the doctrine of Indoor Management is:

Royal British Bank v Turquand (1856):

In this case, the Royal British Bank sued Turquand to recover money lent to the company, alleging that the loan was invalid because the company's articles required a resolution of the shareholders before borrowing. However, the court held that Turquand was entitled to assume that the internal procedures had been followed, as the company's articles were publicly available and did not require him to inquire into the validity of the resolution. This decision laid the foundation for the Indoor Management doctrine, which protects outsiders who rely on the apparent authority of directors and officers of a company.

Another significant case that reaffirmed the principle of Indoor Management is:

Mahony v East Holyford Mining Co. (1875):

In this case, the company's articles required that certain resolutions be passed at general meetings. However, the resolutions were passed at board meetings instead. The court held that outsiders dealing with the company were entitled to assume that the resolutions had been properly passed, even if they were aware of the articles' requirements. This case further solidified the protection afforded to third parties under the doctrine of Indoor Management.

These landmark cases illustrate how the doctrine of Indoor Management operates to protect third parties who transact with a company in good faith, even if the company's internal procedures are not strictly followed. This principle promotes commercial certainty and facilitates business transactions by providing a measure of assurance to outsiders dealing with companies.

Q.11. Discuss the ruels laid down in the important case of Foss v. Harbottle.

Ans. The case of Foss v. Harbottle, which originated in English common law and has had a significant influence on company law jurisprudence, established fundamental principles regarding the ability of shareholders to bring actions on behalf of a company. The case set forth rules that continue to shape the legal landscape concerning derivative actions and the limitations thereof. Here are the key rules laid down in the case:

1. Prohibition on Shareholder Actions: Foss v. Harbottle established the principle that the courts will generally not entertain actions brought by individual shareholders against the company's directors or third parties for wrongs done to the company itself. This is known as the rule in Foss v. Harbottle.

2. Exclusivity of Company's Right to Sue: The case affirmed that the company, as a separate legal entity, possesses its own distinct personality and is entitled to sue and be sued in its own name. Accordingly, where the company suffers harm, the proper plaintiff to bring an action is the company itself, not individual shareholders.

3. Exceptions to the Rule: Despite the general prohibition on shareholder actions, Foss v. Harbottle recognized two exceptions where shareholders can bring derivative actions on behalf of the company:

- Ultra Vires Acts: Shareholders may bring an action if the company has acted beyond its legal powers, such as by undertaking activities not authorized by its memorandum of association.

- Fraud on Minority: Shareholders may sue if the wrongdoers are in control of the company and have perpetrated acts that unfairly prejudice the interests of minority shareholders.

4. Majority Rule: The case emphasized the principle that decisions concerning the company's internal affairs should be made by the majority of shareholders in accordance with the company's articles of association. Courts will generally not interfere with such decisions unless there is evidence of fraud, oppression of minority shareholders, or ultra vires acts.

5. Corporate Governance and Control: Foss v. Harbottle highlighted the importance of corporate governance mechanisms and the role of shareholders in overseeing the actions of directors. It underscored the need for shareholders to exercise their rights through proper corporate channels, such as general meetings and voting resolutions.

Overall, Foss v. Harbottle laid down foundational principles governing shareholder actions and derivative suits, balancing the rights of shareholders with the principles of corporate governance and the separate legal personality of the company. While the case sets clear limitations on shareholder litigation, it also recognizes the need for remedies in exceptional circumstances where the company's interests are at risk due to unlawful or oppressive conduct.

Q.12. Discuss the doctrine of 'ultra vires' in Company Law with reference to cases decided by the Indian Courts.

Ans. The doctrine of ultra vires, derived from Latin, means "beyond the powers." In company law, this doctrine refers to actions taken by a company that are beyond the scope of its memorandum of association (MOA). If a company engages in activities or enters into contracts that are beyond the objects specified in its MOA, those actions are considered ultra vires and, therefore, void and unenforceable.

In India, the doctrine of ultra vires plays a crucial role in ensuring that companies operate within the limits of their stated objectives and do not exceed their authorized powers. Several cases decided by Indian courts have helped to shape and reinforce this doctrine. Here are a few notable examples:

1. Ashbury Railway Carriage and Iron Co. Ltd. v. Riche (1875):
- In this landmark case, the House of Lords in England established the principle of ultra vires. The Ashbury Railway Company had entered into a contract to lend money for the construction of railway lines in Belgium, which was beyond the scope of its objects clause in the MOA. The House of Lords held that the company's actions were ultra vires and, therefore, void.

2. Satyabrata Ghose v. Mugneeram Bangur & Co. (1954):
- In this Indian case, the Supreme Court reaffirmed the doctrine of ultra vires. The court held that any transaction entered into by a company that falls outside the scope of its MOA is void and cannot be ratified by the shareholders, even if they unanimously agree.

3. Jyoti Brothers v. Nanalal Zaver & Co. (1965):
- In this case, the Bombay High Court held that if a company's directors enter into a contract that is ultra vires, the company cannot enforce it against the other party. However, if the other party was aware of the company's limitations, they cannot take advantage of the ultra vires doctrine to escape their obligations.

4. Hindustan Industrial Chemicals Ltd. v. State of Assam (1967):
- This case involved a company that had exceeded its authorized borrowing limit as per its MOA. The Supreme Court held that any borrowing beyond the limit specified in the MOA was ultra vires and void, emphasizing the importance of adherence to the objects clause.

5. **Oriental Metal Pressing Works Pvt. Ltd. v. R. K. Behal & Co. (1974)**:
- In this case, the Delhi High Court held that a contract entered into by a company that is ultra vires is void ab initio (from the beginning) and cannot be ratified by the shareholders, directors, or anyone else.

These cases illustrate how the doctrine of ultra vires operates in Indian company law to ensure that companies act within their authorized powers as defined in their MOA. Any action taken beyond these powers is considered void and unenforceable, providing protection to shareholders and stakeholders.

Q.13. What is 'Prospectus'? Who are liable for a misstatment in a prospectus?

Ans. In accordance with The Companies Act 2013, a prospectus is a legal document issued by a company inviting the public to subscribe to its shares or debentures. It contains essential information about the company, its business operations, financial performance, and terms of the securities being offered for subscription. The prospectus serves as a key communication tool between the company and potential investors, providing them with relevant information to make informed investment decisions.

Under Section 34 of The Companies Act 2013, a prospectus must disclose all material facts related to the company and the securities being offered. Any misstatement or omission of material facts in the prospectus can lead to legal consequences for the company and its officers. Section 35 of the Act specifies the liabilities for misstatements in a prospectus. It states that:

1. Civil Liability: If any person subscribes for securities based on a prospectus containing false or misleading statements, they may bring legal action against the company, its directors, promoters, and any other person who authorized the issue of the prospectus. These individuals are jointly and severally liable to compensate the subscriber for any loss or damage suffered as a result of the misstatement.

2. Criminal Liability: Any person who authorizes the issue of a prospectus containing false or misleading statements with the intent to deceive or defraud is subject to criminal prosecution. If found guilty, they may be liable for imprisonment and/or fines.

Case law provides further interpretation and application of these legal provisions. One notable case is Derry v. Peek (1889), which established the principle of fraudulent misrepresentation in prospectuses. In this case, the directors of a tramway company issued a prospectus containing statements about the profitability of the company's operations, which later turned out to be false. The House of Lords held that the directors were liable for fraudulent misrepresentation as they had made false statements knowingly or recklessly, with the intent to deceive investors.

Overall, the prospectus serves as a critical document in the securities offering process, and any misstatement or omission in it can have serious legal consequences for the company and its officers. Investors rely on the accuracy and completeness of the information disclosed in the prospectus to make investment decisions, and the law holds those responsible for any misleading statements or omissions accountable for their actions.

CHAPTER TWO

Labour & Industrial Laws

2023 Question Paper

Q.1. Industrial Disputes.

Ans. In Section 2 (k) of the Industrial Disputes Act, 1947, an "industrial dispute" is defined as any disagreement involving employers and employers, or employers and workers, or workers among themselves, related to employment status, terms of employment, or working conditions of individuals. Resolving such disputes typically involves negotiation, mediation, or arbitration, with the goal of achieving a mutually agreeable solution and fostering positive industrial relations. Skillful management of industrial disputes is crucial for fostering a harmonious workplace atmosphere and sustaining the stability and advancement of the industrial domain.

Q.2. Lay-Off.

Ans. Under Section 2(kkk) of the Industrial Disputes Act, 1947 ("the Act"), a layoff is defined as the situation where an employer is unable, due to circumstances beyond their control, to provide employment to a worker listed in the muster roll of an industrial establishment. Such circumstances may include insufficient resources like coal, power, or raw materials, surplus stock, machinery breakdown, natural disasters, or any other similar or related reasons.

Q.3. Define Trade Union and discuss multiplicity of Trade Unions.

Ans. A trade union is an organized association of workers or employees formed to protect and promote their collective interests, such as better wages, improved working conditions, and fair treatment by employers. These unions often negotiate with employers on behalf of their members, aiming to secure favorable terms of employment and resolve disputes.

Under the Industrial Disputes Act, 1947, the multiplicity of trade unions refers to the existence of multiple unions representing workers in a particular industry or establishment. Section 9A of the Act addresses this issue by providing for the recognition of trade unions by employers. Here's a discussion on how the Act deals with the multiplicity of trade unions:

1. Recognition: Section 9A allows employers to recognize one or more trade unions as the representative union(s) for collective bargaining purposes. Once recognized, these unions have the authority to negotiate with the employer on behalf of the workers they represent.

2. Procedure for Recognition: The Act outlines the procedure for the recognition of trade unions, which typically involves consultation with representatives of the workers and assessing the union's membership and legitimacy.

3. Avoidance of Multiplicity: Recognizing a single or limited number of trade unions helps avoid the fragmentation of the workforce and promotes more effective collective bargaining. It streamlines the negotiation process and ensures that the interests of the majority of workers are represented.

4. Collective Bargaining: Once recognized, trade unions engage in collective bargaining with employers to negotiate terms and conditions of employment, such as wages, working hours, benefits, and grievance procedures.

5. Dispute Resolution: In case of disputes regarding recognition or representation, the Industrial Disputes Act provides mechanisms for resolution through conciliation, arbitration, or adjudication by labor authorities or tribunals.

Overall, the Industrial Disputes Act, 1947, aims to regulate the multiplicity of trade unions by facilitating the recognition of representative unions and promoting orderly collective bargaining processes to maintain industrial peace and harmony.

Q.4. Basic objects of the Payment of Wages Act, 1936.

Ans. The Payment of Wages Act, 1936 aims to regulate the timely payment of wages to employees and ensure transparency in wage-related transactions. Its basic objectives include:

- Ensuring timely and full payment of wages to employees.
- Preventing unauthorized deductions from wages.
- Prescribing the mode and frequency of wage payments.
- Prohibiting fines and deductions except those specified under the Act.
- Providing recourse to employees for redressal of wage-related grievances through designated authorities.
- Promoting fair and equitable treatment of workers in wage-related matters.

The Act seeks to safeguard the financial interests of employees and promote social justice in the realm of employment.

Q.5. 'Partial disablement' in context of Workmen's Compensation Act, 1923.

Ans. Under the Workmen's Compensation Act, 1923, "partial disablement" refers to a condition where a worker suffers a loss of earning capacity due to an injury or occupational disease incurred during the course of employment. The Act provides compensation for both total and partial disablement of workers.

The relevant sections of the Workmen's Compensation Act, 1923, pertaining to partial disablement are Sections 2(1)(g) and 4.

1. Section 2(1)(g): This section defines "partial disablement" as the loss of earning capacity of a worker resulting from an employment injury. It specifies that partial disablement does not include permanent disablement resulting from the injury or occupational disease.

2. Section 4: This section outlines the compensation payable for temporary and permanent disablement, including partial disablement. It provides a schedule of compensation based on the degree of disablement and the worker's average weekly wages.

Case law examples regarding partial disablement under the Workmen's Compensation Act, 1923, may include:

1. S. Ramanathan vs. Management of South Indian Railway Company (AIR 1968 SC 423): In this case, the Supreme Court of India emphasized that compensation for partial disablement should be awarded based on the degree of loss of earning capacity, considering the nature and extent of the injury and its impact on the worker's ability to work.

2. Shyama Charan Gupta vs. Western Railway (AIR 1981 All 37): This case highlighted the importance of medical evidence in determining the extent of partial disablement and assessing the worker's loss of earning capacity. The court emphasized the need for objective medical examination to ascertain the degree of disablement accurately.

These cases illustrate the legal principles and precedents concerning partial disablement under the Workmen's Compensation Act, 1923, emphasizing the importance of fair compensation based on the worker's actual loss of earning capacity due to the injury or occupational disease.

Q.6. Clearly explain who is a workman of an employer under the Industrial Disputes Act, 1947

Ans. Under the Industrial Disputes Act, 1947, the term "workman" is defined in Section 2(s). It states:

"Workman" means any person (including an apprentice) employed in any industry to do any manual, unskilled, skilled, technical, operational, clerical, or supervisory work for hire or reward, whether the terms of employment be express or implied, and for the purposes of any proceeding under this Act in relation to an industrial dispute, includes any such person who has been dismissed, discharged, or retrenched in connection with, or as a consequence of, that dispute, or whose dismissal, discharge, or retrenchment has led to that dispute, but does not include any such person—

(i) who is subject to the Air Force Act, 1950 (45 of 1950), or the Army Act, 1950 (46 of 1950), or the Navy Act, 1957 (62 of 1957); or

(ii) who is employed in the police service or as an officer or other employee of a prison; or

(iii) who is employed mainly in a managerial or administrative capacity; or

(iv) who, being employed in a supervisory capacity, draws wages exceeding one thousand six hundred rupees per mensem or exercises, either by the nature of the duties attached to the office or by reason of the powers vested in him, functions mainly of a managerial nature.

This definition is crucial for determining who falls within the scope of protection and representation under the Act. It covers a wide range of employees engaged in various types of work, excluding certain categories such as those in managerial or administrative roles.

Case law, such as the landmark decision in Bangalore Water Supply and Sewerage Board vs. A. Rajappa and Others (1978), has provided further interpretation and clarification of the term "workman" under the Industrial Disputes Act. In this case, the Supreme Court held that the term "workman" should be interpreted broadly to include all categories of workers who contribute to the production process, regardless of their skill level or the nature of their work. The court emphasized the need to interpret the Act in a manner that promotes social justice and protects the interests of workers.

Overall, the definition of "workman" under the Industrial Disputes Act, 1947, is comprehensive and inclusive, encompassing a wide range of employees engaged in industrial activities, while also providing exceptions for certain categories of workers.

Q.7. Discuss the procedure for the registration and recognition of a Trade Union.

Ans. The procedure for the registration and recognition of a trade union is outlined in the Trade Unions Act, 1926. Here's a discussion of the procedure along with relevant sections and case law:

1. Registration of Trade Union:

- Section 4 of the Trade Unions Act, 1926, lays down the procedure for the registration of a trade union. According to this section, any seven or more members of a trade union may apply for its registration.

- The application for registration must be made to the Registrar of Trade Unions appointed by the appropriate government.

- The application must be accompanied by a copy of the rules of the trade union and a statement of the names, occupations, and addresses of the members making the application.

2. Consideration of Application:

- Section 5 of the Act requires the Registrar to consider the application and ensure that it complies with the requirements of the Act.

- The Registrar may call for further information or clarification if necessary.

- Once satisfied, the Registrar registers the trade union and issues a certificate of registration.

3. Effect of Registration:

- Section 6 provides that a registered trade union shall be a body corporate by the name under which it is registered and shall have perpetual succession and a common seal.

- It can sue and be sued in its registered name and acquire and hold movable and immovable property.

4. **Recognition of Trade Union:**

- While registration under the Trade Unions Act confers certain legal benefits, recognition by the employer provides the union with the right to represent the workers for collective bargaining purposes.

- Section 9A of the Industrial Disputes Act, 1947, deals with the recognition of trade unions by employers.

- Employers may recognize one or more trade unions as representative unions for collective bargaining.

5. Case Law:

- In the case of Bijay Cotton Mills Ltd. v. State of Ajmer, the Supreme Court held that the requirements for registration under the Trade Unions Act must be strictly complied with. Any non-compliance can render the registration invalid.

- In Kameshwar Prasad v. The State of Bihar, the court emphasized that the Registrar must exercise discretion in considering applications for registration and should not refuse registration arbitrarily.

Overall, the registration and recognition of a trade union involve adherence to the procedural requirements specified in the Trade Unions Act, 1926, and relevant provisions of other labor laws. Compliance with these procedures ensures the legal recognition and protection of the rights of trade unions and their members.

Q.8. Explain the contribution under Employees Provident Fund Act, 1991.

Ans. The Employees Provident Fund Act, 1951, imposes a statutory obligation on employers to contribute to the Employees' Provident Fund (EPF) for the benefit of their employees. This contribution, as outlined in relevant sections of the Act, serves multiple purposes:

1. Retirement Savings (Section 6):*The contributions made by employers help employees accumulate savings for their post-employment years, ensuring financial security and stability during retirement.

2. Social Security (Section 7): The EPF contribution acts as a form of social security, providing employees with a safety net during times of financial distress, such as unemployment, disability, or medical emergencies.

3. Employee Welfare (Section 2): The Act promotes the welfare of employees by fostering long-term savings habits and facilitating access to funds for various life events, including housing, education, or medical expenses.

4. Employer Obligation (Section 6): Employers are legally obligated to make contributions to the EPF on behalf of their employees. This obligation underscores the employer's responsibility to safeguard the financial well-being and retirement planning of their workforce.

Case Law:

*In the case of **Bridge and Roof Co. (India) Ltd. v. Union of India**, the Supreme Court held that the EPF contribution is a vital aspect of the Employees Provident Fund Act, 1951, aimed at ensuring the financial security and welfare of employees. The court emphasized the importance of strict compliance by employers with their contribution obligations under the Act to uphold the rights and benefits of employees.*

Thus, the contribution mandated by the Employees Provident Fund Act, 1951, plays a pivotal role in promoting financial stability, social security, and employee welfare, thereby fulfilling the objectives of the Act.

Q.9. Give a brief account of evolution of 'Industrial Legislation' in India.

Ans. The evolution of industrial legislation in India can be traced back to the colonial era, where the British introduced various labor laws to regulate industrial relations and protect the interests of workers. The Factory Act of 1881 was one of the earliest pieces of legislation aimed at regulating working conditions in factories, followed by subsequent enactments such as the Workmen's Compensation Act of 1923, which provided for compensation to workers for injuries suffered during employment.

Post-independence, there was a significant expansion of labor laws to address the social and economic needs of the newly independent nation. The Industrial Disputes Act of 1947 was enacted to provide mechanisms for the resolution of disputes between employers and employees, while the Minimum Wages Act of 1948 aimed to ensure fair remuneration for workers. The scope and coverage of industrial legislation in India have continued to evolve, with the introduction of laws addressing issues such as occupational safety, health, welfare, and social security of workers. Key enactments include the Employees' Provident Funds and Miscellaneous Provisions Act of 1952, the Payment of Gratuity Act of 1972, and the Employees' State Insurance Act of 1948.

Q.10. When wages of workmen have to be paid in case of strike? When can services of a workman be terminated in case of strike?

Ans. The disbursement of wages to workmen and the cessation of their services hinge upon the particular circumstances and provisions delineated within relevant labor laws and employment agreements.

Payment of Wages (Payment of Wages Act, 1936): Typically, workmen engaged in a lawful strike are entitled to remuneration for the period they were available for work but were unable to engage due to the strike. However, they may not be eligible for wages during the actual duration of the strike itself. The Payment of Wages Act, 1936, along with other pertinent regulations, oversee the payment of wages during strikes, furnishing employers with directives to adhere to in such scenarios.

Termination of Services: The cessation of a workman's employment during a strike may transpire under specific circumstances. This includes instances where the strike is deemed unlawful or if the workman is found engaging in misconduct or violence throughout the strike period. Employers also reserve the right to terminate the services of workmen if the strike precipitates an extended disruption of business operations or if alternate arrangements cannot be made to ensure the uninterrupted provision of essential services.

Relevant Case Law:

In Central Inland Water Transport Corporation Ltd. and Another v. Brojo Nath Ganguly and Another, the Supreme Court underscored the significance of adhering to due process and statutory provisions when terminating the services of employees, even during a strike. The court emphasized that arbitrary or unjustified terminations would contravene labor laws and could lead to legal repercussions.

Navigating the intricacies of wage payment and service termination during strikes necessitates a comprehensive understanding of pertinent legal frameworks, employment contracts, and industrial relations conventions. Employers and workmen are encouraged to seek legal counsel and observe due diligence to effectively address any disputes or challenges arising from strikes while upholding the principles of fairness and legal compliance.

Q.11. Discuss the immunities from civil and criminal liabilities available to the office bearers or a Trade Union.

Ans. Trade union office bearers benefit from specific immunities from both civil and criminal liabilities, crucial for ensuring the smooth operation of trade unions and the safeguarding of their members' interests. These immunities are designed to protect the rights of trade union officials to advocate for their members without fear of legal repercussions.

Civil Immunities:

Under Section 17 of the Trade Unions Act, 1926, trade union office bearers are generally shielded from civil liabilities for actions conducted in good faith and within the scope of their duties. This protection guards them against personal liability for any damages or losses resulting from their activities while representing the trade union or its members. However, this immunity does not cover actions that are fraudulent, malicious, or beyond the authority granted to them.

Case Law:

In the case of Chinnaya v. Ramaya, the Madras High Court ruled that trade union officials are immune from civil liabilities as long as their actions are undertaken in good faith and within the framework of their responsibilities. This decision reinforced the principle that civil immunities are essential for the effective functioning of trade unions.

Criminal Immunities:

Similarly, trade union office bearers enjoy immunity from criminal liabilities under Section 120B of the Indian Penal Code for acts committed in the lawful pursuit of their official duties. This protection shields them from prosecution for offenses such as defamation, conspiracy, or intimidation arising during trade union activities, provided that their actions are legal and aligned with trade union objectives.

Case Law:

In the case of M. K. Raja v. M. R. Raja, the Kerala High Court affirmed that trade union office bearers are entitled to immunity from criminal prosecution if their actions are undertaken in furtherance of their trade union duties and objectives. This ruling emphasized the importance of criminal immunities in safeguarding trade union activities.

To sum up, these immunities are indispensable for preserving the autonomy and effectiveness of trade unions in advocating for their members' rights, promoting collective bargaining, and maintaining harmonious industrial relations. However, it is crucial to ensure a balance between these immunities and accountability to prevent their abuse and ensure compliance with the law.

Q.12. Define deduction. When deductions can be made by an employer from the wages of an employee under the Payment of Wages Act, 1936.

Ans.

In the realm of employment law, a deduction pertains to the withholding or reduction of a certain amount from an employee's wages by the employer for various reasons. The Payment of Wages Act, 1936, governs the payment of wages to employees and lays down guidelines regarding when deductions can be made by an employer.

Section 7 of the Payment of Wages Act permits deductions from an employee's wages under specific circumstances, which include:

1. Deductions for Fines (Section 8): Employers are authorized to deduct fines from an employee's wages for acts of misconduct or breaches of discipline, subject to certain conditions. The total fines imposed in any wage period

should not exceed an amount equal to three percent of the wages payable to the employee.

2. Deductions for Absence from Duty (Section 9): Employers can make deductions for periods during which an employee is absent from duty without permission, as per the terms and conditions specified in the employment contract or company policies.

3. Deductions for Damage or Loss (Section 10): Employers have the right to deduct amounts from an employee's wages to recover the costs of damage or loss caused by the employee's negligence or willful misconduct. However, the employee must be given an opportunity to contest such deductions.

4. Other Statutory Deductions: Employers may also make deductions mandated by law, such as deductions for income tax, provident fund contributions, or other statutory deductions required by government authorities.

It's imperative to adhere to the provisions of the Payment of Wages Act and any other relevant laws or regulations while making deductions. Unauthorized or excessive deductions can lead to legal disputes and penalties for the employer.

Regarding relevant case law, **State of Bombay v. Hospital Mazdoor Sabha** (AIR 1960 SC 610) is significant. In this case, the Supreme Court held that deductions made by an employer must comply with the provisions of the Payment of Wages Act, and any attempt to make unauthorized deductions is impermissible under the law.

Q.13. What do you understand by Maternity Benefit? For what period a woman employee shall be entitled to maternity benefit under the Maternity Benefit Act, 1961?

Ans. Maternity Benefit refers to the provisions made by employers or the government to provide financial assistance and job security to women employees during their pregnancy and after childbirth. It's aimed at ensuring that pregnant women can take adequate rest before and after childbirth without worrying about job security or financial stability.

In India, the Maternity Benefit Act, 1961, provides for maternity benefits to women employees. According to Section 5 of the Act, a woman employee shall be entitled to maternity benefit for a maximum period of 26 weeks. This includes:

1. Before childbirth: Up to eight weeks of maternity leave before the expected date of delivery.
2. After childbirth: Up to 18 weeks of maternity leave after the delivery.

However, in case of complications arising due to pregnancy, miscarriage, or medical termination, a woman can avail an extension of her leave up to one month. This is provided under Section 10 of the Act.

In the case of "Punjab National Bank vs. Presiding Officer" (2001), the Supreme Court of India held that the purpose of maternity benefits is to ensure the health of the mother and the child. The court emphasized the importance of granting maternity leave and benefits as a fundamental right and upheld the provisions of the Maternity Benefit Act, 1961.

Moreover, the Act also provides other benefits such as nursing breaks for women employees to breastfeed their child. These provisions are essential for promoting gender equality in the workforce and ensuring the well-being of both mother and child.

2022 Question Paper

Q.1. When is Individual Dispute deemed to be an Industrial dispute under the Industrial Disputes Act, 1947.

Ans. An individual dispute is deemed to be an industrial dispute under the Industrial Disputes Act, 1947, when it pertains to a dispute or difference between an employer and an individual worker, or between individual workers, which is connected with the employment or non-employment, or the terms of employment, or with the conditions of labor, of any person. Essentially, if the dispute has implications beyond the individual level and affects the industrial relations or interests of a group of workers or the employer-employee relationship within an industry, it is considered an industrial dispute under the Act.

Q.2. Explain Lock-out.

Ans. A lock-out is a temporary cessation of work by an employer or a temporary refusal by an employer to continue to employ any number of workers in an industry. It is a preemptive measure taken by the employer in response to industrial disputes or disagreements with employees' unions. During a lock-out, employees are prevented from accessing the workplace and performing their duties. Lock-outs are typically initiated by employers to exert pressure on employees or their representatives during negotiations or to address issues such as labor disputes, demands for increased wages, or disagreements over working conditions.

Q.3. Role of Outsiders in Trade Union.

Ans. Outsiders play a significant role in trade unions by offering fresh perspectives, expertise, and support. They can provide valuable insights into industry practices, legal matters, and negotiation strategies. Additionally, outsiders bring diverse skills and resources that enhance the effectiveness of union activities, such as organizing campaigns and advocacy efforts. Their involvement can also foster alliances with other stakeholders, amplifying the union's voice and influence. Managing the balance between insider and outsider participation is crucial to maintain the union's autonomy and credibility. The outsiders contribute vital expertise and support, enriching the collective efforts of trade unions.

Q.4. 'Wages' under the Payment of Wager Act, 1936.

Ans. The Payment of Wages Act, 1936, defines 'wages' broadly, covering remuneration for work done, including bonuses, commissions, and allowances. However, it explicitly excludes certain categories like bonus, contributions to pension and provident funds, traveling allowances, and gratuities. This definition aims to ensure that workers receive fair compensation for their labor while delineating specific components that are not considered part of wages for the purpose of the act. Such clarity helps in preventing exploitation and ensures that workers are adequately compensated for their efforts in accordance with the provisions of the Act.

Q.5. 'Dependant' under the Workmen's Compensation Act 1923.

Ans. Under the Workmen's Compensation Act of 1923, the term 'dependent' refers to individuals who rely on the deceased worker for financial support. Dependents can include spouses, children (including adopted and legitimate), and other relatives who were wholly or partially dependent on the deceased's earnings at the time of their death. The Act aims to provide compensation to such dependents for the loss of support resulting from the worker's death due to employment-related injuries or illnesses. The definition of 'dependent' is crucial in determining eligibility for compensation benefits, ensuring that those who rely on the deceased worker are adequately supported.

Q.6. Define Retrenchment. Discuss the procedure under the Section 25 G & 25 H of Industrial Disputes Act, 1947.

Ans. Retrenchment refers to the termination of employment by an employer for reasons such as surplus manpower, economic downturn, or technological advancements. According to Sections 25G and 25H of the Industrial Disputes Act, 1947, certain procedures must be followed before retrenching workers in establishments with over 100 employees. This includes providing a notice to the appropriate government authority and the affected employees, specifying reasons for retrenchment and offering compensation. If ten or more workers are to be retrenched, the employer must also provide prior permission from the government, ensuring fair treatment and mitigating the adverse impact of retrenchment on workers.

Q.7. Discuss the rights of a registered Trade Union.

Ans. A registered trade union enjoys several rights, including legal recognition, collective bargaining, and representation of workers' interests. It can negotiate with employers on behalf of its members regarding wages, working conditions, and other employment-related matters. Additionally, a registered union has the right to participate in industrial disputes resolution processes, including conciliation and arbitration. It can also engage in activities such as organizing strikes, picketing, and peaceful demonstrations to advance workers' rights and interests. Furthermore, a registered trade union is entitled to certain privileges, such as immunity from civil suits for actions taken in good faith in furtherance of trade union objectives, ensuring its autonomy and efficacy in representing workers.

What are the provisions regarding payment of maternity benefit in case of death of a Woman under the Maternity Benefit Act, 1961?

Ans. In the event of a woman's death during her maternity leave period under the Maternity Benefit Act, 1961, certain provisions ensure the continuation of maternity benefits to her nominee or legal heir. If the woman dies before receiving maternity benefits, the employer must pay the amount due to her nominee or legal representative. The nominee could be her husband, or if there is no husband or he is not alive, any other person appointed by her. This payment includes the maternity benefit for the entire period she was entitled to, up to the date of her death. The Act mandates that the employer pays this amount within 48 hours of receiving the notice of the woman's death. Such provisions aim to ensure that the woman's entitlements under the Maternity Benefit Act are not lost and are extended to her nominee or legal heir, providing financial support during a difficult time.

Define Industry. Discuss with the help of decided cases.

Ans. The term "industry" has been broadly defined under various labor legislations and judicial interpretations. In the context of labor laws, it typically encompasses any systematic activity organized for the production or distribution of goods or services.

Several decided cases have contributed to clarifying the definition of "industry." Notably, in the landmark case of Bangalore Water Supply & Sewerage Board v. A. Rajappa (1978), the Supreme Court of India held that an "industry" involves systematic and organized activity involving cooperation between employers and employees to produce goods or services, whether for profit or not. This decision expanded the scope of the term beyond traditional manufacturing sectors to include essential services and public utilities.

In Standard Vacuum Refining Co. of India v. Its Workmen (1960), the court emphasized that an industry is not limited to activities aimed at profit-making but also encompasses charitable, philanthropic, and educational institutions where systematic work is carried out by cooperation between employers and employees.

These cases underscore the broad and inclusive nature of the term "industry," encompassing a wide range of organized activities aimed at production or distribution, irrespective of profit motives, thereby ensuring comprehensive coverage under labor laws.

Discuss the scope, Object and Main Features of the Industrial Disputes Act, 1947

Ans. The Industrial Disputes Act, 1947, is a cornerstone legislation in India regulating labor relations and resolving disputes in industrial establishments. Its scope extends to all industries, covering both organized and unorganized sectors. The Act's primary objective is to promote industrial peace and harmony by providing mechanisms for the amicable settlement of disputes between employers and employees. It seeks to ensure fair and just conditions of employment, prevent unfair labor practices, and protect workers' rights.

Key features of the Act include the recognition of trade unions, which allows workers to collectively bargain with employers, and the provision of settlement mechanisms such as conciliation, arbitration, and adjudication by labor courts or tribunals. It prohibits unfair labor practices, victimization of workers, and lays down regulations for strikes and lockouts, balancing the interests of both parties while maintaining industrial peace.

The Industrial Disputes Act, 1947, serves as a vital framework for fostering healthy industrial relations and safeguarding workers' interests in India.

Discuss Collective Bargaining and Growth of Trade Unions in India.

Ans. Collective bargaining is a process whereby representatives of workers, usually trade unions, negotiate with employers to reach agreements on various terms and conditions of employment. In India, collective bargaining plays a significant role in shaping labor relations and ensuring the protection of workers' rights.

The growth of trade unions in India has been closely intertwined with the evolution of collective bargaining. Initially, trade unions emerged primarily in response to the exploitation and harsh working conditions faced by workers during the colonial period. Over time, trade unions gained recognition and became influential voices advocating for workers' rights and welfare.

The Trade Unions Act of 1926 provided legal recognition to trade unions, further facilitating their growth and organization. Subsequent labor legislations, such as the Industrial Disputes Act of 1947, strengthened the role of trade unions by providing mechanisms for collective bargaining and dispute resolution.

The growth of trade unions in India has been influenced by various factors, including economic and social changes, industrialization, globalization, and government policies. While trade unions have faced challenges such as fragmentation, political interference, and declining membership in certain sectors, they continue to play a crucial role in representing workers' interests and negotiating better terms and conditions of employment through collective bargaining.

Collective bargaining and the growth of trade unions in India have contributed to improving labor standards, ensuring social justice, and fostering a more equitable workplace environment.

Discuss the object and relevance of the Employees Provident Fund Scheme.

Ans. The Employees Provident Fund (EPF) Scheme is a social security measure introduced in India with the objective of providing financial security and stability to employees post-retirement. Its primary aim is to encourage savings among employees during their working years, ensuring that they have a source of income after retirement.

One of the key objectives of the EPF Scheme is to build a corpus through mandatory contributions from both employees and employers. These contributions accumulate over time and earn interest, creating a retirement fund for employees. Upon retirement, employees can withdraw the accumulated amount or receive a monthly pension, depending on their preferences.

The EPF Scheme also serves as a safety net for employees during emergencies by allowing partial withdrawals for specific purposes such as medical treatment, education, housing, or marriage.

Moreover, the EPF Scheme promotes financial inclusion and discipline among the workforce by encouraging regular savings. It ensures that employees have a reliable source of income during their retirement years, reducing their dependence on family or social welfare programs.

The EPF Scheme is relevant because it addresses the long-term financial needs of employees, promotes social security, and contributes to their overall well-being, thereby fostering economic stability and social development in the country.

Explain the extent of the liability of an employer to compensate the employees under the Workmen's Compensation Act, 1923.

Ans. The Workmen's Compensation Act, 1923, imposes a statutory liability on employers to compensate employees for injuries or death arising out of and in the course of employment. The extent of this liability is determined based on the severity of the injury, the nature of employment, and the employee's wages.

The Act provides for two types of compensation:

Compensation for temporary disablement: If an employee suffers a temporary disability due to a work-related injury, the employer is liable to pay a weekly compensation equal to a certain percentage of the employee's wages, subject to a maximum limit prescribed by the Act. This compensation is payable until the disability ceases or until the employee resumes work, whichever is earlier.

Compensation for permanent disablement or death: In case of permanent disablement or death of an employee due to a work-related injury, the Act provides for a lump sum compensation. The amount of compensation varies based on the nature and extent of the disability or the number of dependents in case of death.

The Act imposes strict liability on employers, regardless of whether the injury or death was due to the employer's negligence. However, certain defenses are available to employers, such as contributory negligence on the part of the employee or the employee's willful disobedience of safety regulations.

The Workmen's Compensation Act, 1923, ensures that employees are adequately compensated for work-related injuries or death, thereby promoting their welfare and providing financial security to them and their dependents.

2019 Question Paper

Q.1. Explain Lock-out

Ans. In the context of labor laws, the regulation of lock-outs typically falls under statutes governing industrial disputes and collective bargaining. Here are sections from relevant labor laws along with a case law example:

1. Industrial Disputes Act, 1947:

- Section 2(oo): Defines "lock-out" as the temporary closing of a place of employment, or the suspension of work, or the refusal by an employer to continue to employ any number of persons employed by them.

- Section 22: Provides provisions for the legality and procedures for declaring a lock-out.

- Section 23: Specifies the conditions under which a lock-out may be deemed illegal.

2. Trade Union Act, 1926:

- Section 24: Addresses the legality and consequences of a lock-out during an industrial dispute.

3. Case Law Example:

- Bangalore Water Supply and Sewerage Board v. A. Rajappa and Others (1978): In this case, the Supreme Court of India discussed the legality of a lock-out declared by the Bangalore Water Supply and Sewerage Board during an industrial dispute. The court emphasized the importance of adhering to the procedures and conditions laid down in the Industrial Disputes Act, 1947, for declaring a lock-out. It held that a lock-out declared without complying with the statutory provisions could be deemed illegal and subjected the employer to legal consequences, including payment of compensation to affected employees.

Lock-outs, as defensive measures by employers during industrial disputes, are subject to legal scrutiny and regulation to ensure fair labor practices and industrial harmony. Compliance with statutory provisions and adherence to procedural requirements are essential for the legality of a lock-out and to avoid legal repercussions for employers.

Q.2. What is the remedy if the registration of a trade-union is refused?

Ans. If the registration of a trade union is refused by the appropriate authority, the trade union has the right to appeal against the refusal. The remedy available is to file an appeal to the higher authority or the concerned government department, tribunal, or court within the stipulated time frame as per the provisions of the relevant trade union legislation. The appeal process allows the trade union to present its case and challenge the reasons for the refusal of registration. If the appeal is successful, the trade union may be granted registration, enabling it to enjoy legal recognition and exercise its rights under the law.

Q.3. What is the time for payment of wages?

Ans. The time for payment of wages is typically stipulated by labor laws or employment contracts and varies depending on the jurisdiction and industry. In many countries, including India, labor laws require employers to pay wages at regular intervals, such as weekly, bi-weekly, or monthly. The exact time for payment of wages may also be specified in collective bargaining agreements or employment contracts negotiated between employers and employees or their representatives. Timely payment of wages ensures financial stability for workers and compliance with legal requirements, contributing to labor relations and employee satisfaction. Failure to pay wages on time may result in legal penalties or disputes.

Q.4. What is the penalty for contravention of the Maternity Benefit Act, 1961 by employer?

Ans. Employers who contravene the Maternity Benefit Act, 1961, may face penalties as per the provisions of the Act. The penalty for non-compliance or contravention typically includes fines, which can vary depending on the nature and severity of the offense. Additionally, repeated violations may lead to more severe penalties, such as imprisonment of the employer or closure of the establishment. The Act aims to ensure the protection of women employees during pregnancy and maternity, and penalties serve as deterrents to ensure compliance with the law, safeguarding the rights and welfare of women workers.

Q.5. Is strike a constitutional right? Briefly explain?

Ans. In many democratic countries, including India, the right to strike is often considered a constitutional right, albeit with certain limitations. While the Constitution may not explicitly mention the right to strike, it is often interpreted as an inherent aspect of the freedom of association and expression guaranteed by the Constitution. However, this right is not absolute and may be subject to certain restrictions, such as ensuring public order, protecting essential services, and balancing the rights of workers with the interests of employers and the general public. Courts often play a crucial role in interpreting and upholding the right to strike within the framework of constitutional principles.

Q.6. Write a short note on 'employees entitlement for compensation' and 'the amount of compensation' under the Workman (Employee's) Compensation Act, 1923.

Ans. The Workmen's Compensation Act, 1923, provides a legal framework for compensating employees for injuries or death arising out of and in the course of employment. Under this Act, employees are entitled to compensation for work-related injuries or death, irrespective of fault.

The amount of compensation is determined based on several factors, including the nature and extent of the injury, the employee's wages, and the degree of disability. For temporary disablement, the Act provides for weekly compensation equal to a certain percentage of the employee's wages, payable until the disability ceases or the employee resumes work. In cases of permanent disability or death, the Act prescribes a lump sum compensation amount, which varies based on the extent of the disability or the number of dependents in the case of death.

The Workmen's Compensation Act ensures that employees receive fair and adequate compensation for injuries or death sustained in the course of employment, providing financial support and security to them and their families.

Q.7. Define 'Factory and Industrial establishment' under Payment of Wages Act, 1936. Also give the difference between both.

Ans. Under the Payment of Wages Act, 1936, a "factory" is defined as any premises, including the precincts thereof, where manufacturing process is carried out, and wherein twenty or more workers are employed, or were employed on any day of the preceding twelve months. On the other hand, an "industrial establishment" refers to any establishment, including offices, that is not a factory but where work is carried out and workers are employed, and is either wholly or mainly engaged in industry.

The key difference between a factory and an industrial establishment lies in the nature of the activities conducted therein. Factories are primarily engaged in manufacturing processes with twenty or more workers, whereas industrial establishments encompass a broader range of activities beyond manufacturing, including service industries and offices. Additionally, factories are subject to specific regulations under labor laws due to the nature of their operations, while industrial establishments may be governed by different sets of rules and regulations depending on the nature of their business activities.

Q.8. Write in brief the salient features of Indian Maternity Benefit Act, 1961.

Ans. The Indian Maternity Benefit Act, 1961, is a legislation aimed at promoting the welfare of pregnant women and ensuring their protection during pregnancy and childbirth. Its salient features include:

1. <u>Maternity leave</u>: The Act mandates a minimum of 26 weeks of maternity leave for women working in establishments with ten or more employees. This includes eight weeks of leave before childbirth and eighteen weeks of leave after childbirth.
2. <u>Payment during maternity leave</u>: The Act requires employers to pay the employee during her maternity leave at the rate of her average daily wage for the period of her absence.
3. <u>Medical bonus</u>: Employers are required to provide a medical bonus to pregnant employees who are entitled to maternity benefit under the Act.
4. <u>Prohibition of dismissal</u>: The Act prohibits employers from dismissing or discharging a woman during her maternity leave period.
5. <u>Other provisions</u>: The Act also includes provisions for nursing breaks, maternity protection for adoptive and commissioning mothers, and the appointment of Inspectors for enforcement of the Act.

The Maternity Benefit Act, 1961, aims to ensure the health, safety, and welfare of pregnant women in the workplace, promoting gender equality and maternity protection.

Q.9. Discuss the employer's liability to pay compensation under the Workmen's Compensation Act, 1923.

Ans. The Workmen's Compensation Act, 1923, imposes a strict liability on employers to compensate employees for injuries or death arising out of and in the course of employment, regardless of fault or negligence. This liability extends to all workers employed in industrial establishments, including factories, mines, and construction sites.

Employers are obligated to provide compensation for various types of injuries, including those resulting in temporary or permanent disablement, as well as fatal accidents. The Act specifies the quantum of compensation based on factors such as the nature and extent of the injury, the employee's wages, and the degree of disability.

The Act provides for weekly compensation equal to a percentage of the employee's wages, payable until the disability ceases or the employee resumes work. For permanent disablement or death, the Act prescribes a lump sum compensation amount, which varies based on the extent of the disability or the number of dependents in the case of death.

Employers are required to provide compensation promptly and are prohibited from making any deductions from the compensation amount. Failure to comply with the provisions of the Act may result in legal penalties, including fines and imprisonment, highlighting the significance of employers' liability to pay compensation under the Act in ensuring the welfare and protection of workers.

Q.10. Define 'Industries' under the Industrial Disputes Act, 1947. What are its essential attributes? Whether professions and municipal corporations come under the ambit of the term 'industry'? Discuss.

Ans. Under the Industrial Disputes Act, 1947, "industry" is defined as any systematic activity carried out for the production of goods or services or the distribution of goods or services to satisfy human needs, conducted with the cooperation of employers and employees for mutual benefit.

The essential attributes of industries, as per the Act, include systematic activity, cooperation between employers and employees, production or distribution of goods or services, and serving human needs. These attributes distinguish industries from other forms of economic or professional activities.

Professions, such as those practiced by doctors, lawyers, or accountants, are generally not considered industries under the Industrial Disputes Act because they typically involve individual service provision rather than systematic production or distribution of goods or services.

Municipal corporations may come under the ambit of the term 'industry' if they engage in systematic activities aimed at providing goods or services to the public, such as sanitation services, water supply, or public transportation. The classification of municipal corporations as industries would depend on the specific nature of their activities and whether they meet the essential attributes outlined in the Industrial Disputes Act. Courts may interpret and apply the definition of 'industry' based on the facts and circumstances of each case.

Q.11. State the provisions of the Payment of Wages Act, 1936 relating to fixation of wages and deductions from wages.

Ans. The Payment of Wages Act, 1936, contains provisions related to the fixation of wages and deductions from wages to ensure timely payment and protect the rights of workers.

1. <u>Fixation of wages</u>:

   - The Act mandates that wages should be paid in legal tender, i.e., currency notes or coins, and should be disbursed on specific intervals, either daily, weekly, fortnightly, or monthly, as determined by the employer.
   - Wages should be paid before the expiry of the 7th or 10th day, depending on the number of employees, following the wage period. In case of termination, wages must be paid within two days.
   - The Act prohibits the payment of wages in kind, except for specified circumstances and with the authorization of the appropriate authority.

2. <u>Deductions from wages</u>:

   - Employers are permitted to make deductions from wages only for specific purposes, such as fines, absence from duty, damage or loss of goods expressly entrusted to the employee, or accommodation provided by the employer.
   - Deductions for fines must not exceed an amount equal to 3% of the wages payable in that wage period.
   - Total deductions, excluding those for fines, must not exceed 75% of the wages earned by the employee.

These provisions aim to ensure timely payment of wages and regulate deductions to prevent exploitation and ensure fair treatment of workers under the Payment of Wages Act, 1936.

Q.12. Give a brief account of the evolution of 'Industrial Legislation in India'.

Ans. The evolution of industrial legislation in India can be traced back to the colonial period when the British government introduced various labor laws to regulate the emerging industrial economy and maintain control over the workforce.

During the late 19th and early 20th centuries, several Acts were enacted to address issues such as working hours, safety, and child labor. The Factories Act, 1881, was the first significant legislation aimed at regulating the conditions of work in factories.

The early 20th century saw the emergence of trade unionism and labor movements, leading to the enactment of the Trade Unions Act, 1926, which provided legal recognition to trade unions.

Post-independence, the Indian government embarked on a series of reforms to address the socio-economic challenges facing the country. The Industrial Disputes Act, 1947, was enacted to regulate industrial relations and provide mechanisms for the settlement of disputes between employers and employees.

Subsequent decades witnessed the enactment of various labor laws, including the Minimum Wages Act, 1948, the Payment of Wages Act, 1936, and the Employees' Provident Funds and Miscellaneous Provisions Act, 1952, aimed at protecting the rights and welfare of workers and promoting industrial harmony.

The evolution of industrial legislation in India reflects the country's commitment to ensuring social justice, promoting labor welfare, and fostering harmonious industrial relations.

13. Write short notes on any two of the following-

a. Closure

Ans. Labour and industrial laws are essential legal frameworks that govern relations between employers and employees, ensuring fair treatment, protection of rights, and promoting industrial harmony. These laws cover a wide range of aspects, including wages, working conditions, safety, employment contracts, trade unions, and dispute resolution. By providing guidelines for employment practices, preventing exploitation, and facilitating conflict resolution, labour and industrial laws contribute to creating a conducive environment for sustainable economic growth and social development. They play a crucial role in balancing the interests of employers, employees, and society, fostering a fair and equitable workplace for all stakeholders.

b. Employees Provident Fund

Ans. The Employees' Provident Fund (EPF) is a social security scheme in India aimed at providing financial security and stability to employees post-retirement. Under this scheme, both employees and employers contribute a certain percentage of the employee's salary towards a provident fund account managed by the Employees' Provident Fund Organization (EPFO). The accumulated funds earn interest and serve as a retirement corpus for employees. Withdrawals are permitted for specific purposes such as retirement, marriage, education, or housing. The EPF scheme ensures long-term savings, financial stability, and social security for employees, promoting their overall welfare and well-being.

c. Collective Bargaining

Ans. Collective bargaining is a fundamental right under labor and industrial laws, enabling workers to negotiate with employers collectively through their unions. It involves discussions and agreements on terms and conditions of employment, wages, benefits, and working conditions. Collective bargaining promotes fair labor practices, fosters cooperation between labor and management, and contributes to resolving disputes amicably. It empowers workers to advocate for their rights, ensures better working conditions, and strengthens industrial relations. Through collective bargaining, both employers and employees collaborate to reach mutually beneficial agreements, enhancing productivity and promoting a harmonious workplace environment.

d. Lay-off & Lockout

Ans. Lay-off refers to the temporary suspension or reduction of work by an employer due to reasons such as lack of orders, shortage of materials, or financial constraints. During a lay-off, employees are not provided with work or wages but remain on the employer's payroll.

Lockout, on the other hand, is a defensive measure taken by an employer to shut down operations temporarily, preventing employees from working. It is typically initiated during labor disputes or strikes to exert pressure on employees or unions to accept the employer's terms. Lockouts can result in economic losses for both parties and disrupt industrial peace.

2018 Question Paper

Q.1. Workman.

Ans. According to Section 2(s) of the Industrial Disputes Act, a "Workman" is defined as follows:

A workman encompasses any individual, including an apprentice, engaged in any industry to perform manual, unskilled, skilled technical, operational, clerical, or supervisory work for hire or reward. This definition encompasses individuals whose terms of employment are either explicitly stated or implied. Furthermore, for the purposes of any legal proceedings under this Act related to an industrial dispute, the term "workman" also includes individuals who have been dismissed, discharged, or retrenched in connection with, or as a consequence of, that dispute, or whose dismissal, discharge, or retrenchment has sparked the dispute.

However, the definition of "workman" excludes certain categories of individuals:

1. Those subject to the Air Force Act, 1950 (45 of 1950), the Army Act, 1950 (46 of 1950), or the Navy Act, 1957 (62 of 1957).

2. Individuals employed in the police service or as officers or employees of a prison.

3. Those primarily employed in managerial or administrative capacities.

4. Individuals employed in a supervisory capacity who earn wages exceeding ten thousand rupees per month or who primarily perform managerial duties due to the nature of their job or the powers vested in them.

This definition delineates the scope of individuals covered under the Industrial Disputes Act, ensuring clarity and specificity in the application of labor laws.

Q.2. Appropriate Government.

Ans. As per Section 2(a) of the Industrial Disputes Act, 1947, the term "appropriate government" refers to:

- In relation to industries carried on by or under the authority of the Central Government or by a railway company, mine, oil field, or major port, the appropriate government means the Central Government.

- In relation to any other industry, the appropriate government means the State Government.

This definition delineates the jurisdictional authority responsible for administering and enforcing the provisions of the Industrial Disputes Act based on the nature of the industry and its ownership.

Q.3. Give precedent conditions of retrenchment.

Ans. Precedent conditions of retrenchment typically include situations where the employer needs to downsize due to factors such as surplus manpower, financial constraints, technological advancements, or closure of the establishment. Before retrenching employees, the employer must explore alternatives like redeployment, voluntary retirement schemes, or reducing work hours. Additionally, the employer must adhere to the legal requirements specified in labor laws, including providing notice to employees and obtaining permission from the appropriate government authority if the retrenchment affects a certain number of workers. Retrenchment should be the last resort after considering all viable options and must be conducted fairly and transparently.

Q.4 Whether an educational Institution is an Industry?

Ans. In many cases, educational institutions are not considered industries under labor and industrial laws because their primary purpose is to provide education rather than engage in systematic production or distribution of goods or services. However, the classification may vary depending on the specific activities and operations of the institution. Educational institutions may be classified as industries if they engage in commercial activities such as running vocational courses, providing training services for a fee, or operating profit-oriented ventures. Ultimately, the determination of whether an educational institution qualifies as an industry depends on the nature of its operations and the applicable legal definitions.

Q.5. Court of Inquiry Section-6.

Ans. Section 6 of the Industrial Disputes Act, 1947, empowers the appropriate government to appoint a Court of Inquiry to inquire into any industrial dispute. The Court of Inquiry comprises one or more independent persons with relevant experience or expertise appointed by the government. The purpose of the inquiry is to investigate the causes of the dispute, gather evidence, and make recommendations for its resolution. The Court has the authority to summon witnesses, examine documents, and conduct hearings. Its findings and recommendations are submitted to the government, which may take appropriate action based on the inquiry's report to resolve the dispute.

Q.6. 'Grievance Redressal Committee'. Discuss.

Ans. A Grievance Redressal Committee is a formal mechanism established within organizations to address employee grievances effectively and ensure fair treatment. Comprising representatives from management and employees, the committee provides a platform for employees to voice their concerns, complaints, or dissatisfaction regarding work-related issues. The committee reviews grievances impartially, investigates underlying causes, and works towards finding appropriate solutions or resolutions. By promoting transparency, communication, and conflict resolution, the Grievance Redressal Committee contributes to maintaining a harmonious work environment, enhancing employee satisfaction, and fostering trust between management and employees.

Q.7. When a strike becomes illegal?

Ans. A strike becomes illegal when it violates the provisions of labor laws or specific regulations governing industrial action. This may occur if the strike is undertaken in contravention of procedures outlined in labor laws, such as failure to provide prior notice to the employer or appropriate authorities, or if it disrupts essential services or public order. Strikes can also be deemed illegal if they are declared by unions or employees engaged in prohibited or essential services, as defined by law. Additionally, any strike that involves violence, coercion, or intimidation may be considered illegal, undermining the principles of peaceful industrial action.

Q.8. State the difference between Lay-off & Retrenchment?

Ans. Lay-off and retrenchment are both forms of employment termination, but they differ in their nature and purpose. Lay-off refers to the temporary suspension or reduction of work by an employer due to reasons such as lack of orders, shortage of materials, or financial constraints, with the expectation of re-employment once conditions improve. Retrenchment, on the other hand, involves the permanent termination of employees' services by an employer due to reasons such as surplus manpower, closure of the establishment, or technological advancements, with no immediate expectation of re-employment. While lay-off is temporary, retrenchment is permanent in nature.

Q.9. What is the scope and object of the Industrial Disputes Act, 1947?

Ans. The Industrial Disputes Act, 1947, is a comprehensive legislation aimed at regulating industrial relations and resolving disputes between employers and employees in India. Its scope extends to all industrial establishments, including factories, mines, and plantations, covering both organized and unorganized sectors.

The primary object of the Industrial Disputes Act is to promote industrial peace and harmony by providing mechanisms for the prevention and settlement of disputes arising between employers and employees. It seeks to ensure fair and just conditions of employment, prevent unfair labor practices, and protect the rights of workers.

The Act aims to regulate the process of layoffs, retrenchment, and closure of establishments, safeguarding the interests of workers. It provides for various mechanisms such as conciliation, arbitration, and adjudication by labor courts or tribunals for the resolution of disputes.

The Industrial Disputes Act, 1947, serves to promote social justice, industrial harmony, and the welfare of workers while balancing the interests of employers and employees in the industrial landscape of India.

Q.10. What do you mean by the term Lock out? Is it mandatory to serve a notice before declaring lockout? If so, then under which circumstances it can be waived? Discuss the effect of illegal lockout.

Ans. A lockout refers to the temporary closure or suspension of work by an employer as a defensive measure during an industrial dispute, aiming to prevent employees from working and exert pressure on them or their union to accept the employer's terms. It is a preemptive action undertaken by the employer to protect their interests or negotiate favorable terms.

Under the Industrial Disputes Act, 1947, it is generally mandatory for the employer to serve a notice to the appropriate government authority and the affected employees at least 14 days before declaring a lockout, unless circumstances necessitate immediate action to prevent industrial unrest or for reasons beyond the employer's control.

The requirement for notice can be waived by the appropriate authority in exceptional circumstances, such as threats to public order, natural disasters, or emergencies affecting the establishment's operations.

An illegal lockout occurs when the employer declares a lockout without complying with the legal requirements or during the pendency of conciliation or arbitration proceedings. The effect of an illegal lockout may result in adverse consequences for the employer, including penalties, reinstatement of employees, payment of wages for the lockout period, and even potential civil or criminal liabilities. Additionally, it may escalate tensions and prolong the dispute, damaging labor relations and industrial harmony.

Q.11. What is the procedure for the registration of a Trade Union? How many members are required for the registration of a Trade Union?

Ans. The procedure for the registration of a trade union in India is governed by the Trade Unions Act, 1926. To register a trade union, the following steps must be followed:

Application: The trade union must submit an application to the Registrar of Trade Unions in the state where the union's head office is located. The application must be signed by at least seven members who are eligible for membership under the Act.

Memorandum: The application must be accompanied by a memorandum of association of the trade union containing details such as the name, objectives, and rules of the union.

Rules: The trade union must also submit a copy of its rules, which outline the procedures for membership, meetings, elections, and other organizational matters.

Registration: Upon receipt of the application and documents, the Registrar will scrutinize the same and, if satisfied, register the trade union. Once registered, the union becomes a legal entity with certain rights and obligations.

As per the Trade Unions Act, 1926, a trade union must have a minimum of seven members to be eligible for registration. These members must be workers employed in industries specified in the Act, such as manufacturing, mining, or transport. The Act also specifies that the members must pay a subscription fee to the union for a specified period to demonstrate their commitment to the organization.

Q.12. Define and Discuss in detail 'Industrial Dispute' under the Industrial Dispute Act, 1947.

Ans. An industrial dispute under the Industrial Disputes Act, 1947, refers to any disagreement or conflict between employers and employees or between employees and employees that arises in the course of employment, relating to any industrial matter. This can include disputes over wages, benefits, working conditions, disciplinary actions, termination of employment, or any other issue affecting the terms of employment or the rights of workers.

Industrial disputes can manifest in various forms, such as strikes, lockouts, protests, or grievances raised through formal channels. They may involve collective action by workers or individual grievances brought forth by employees.

The Industrial Disputes Act, 1947, provides a comprehensive framework for the prevention and resolution of industrial disputes. It outlines procedures for conciliation, arbitration, and adjudication by labor courts or tribunals to facilitate the amicable settlement of disputes and promote industrial peace.

The Act also defines the roles and responsibilities of employers, employees, and government authorities in managing industrial disputes, ensuring fair treatment, protecting workers' rights, and maintaining harmonious industrial relations. By providing mechanisms for dispute resolution and promoting dialogue between the parties involved, the Act aims to prevent disruptions to production, safeguard the interests of both employers and employees, and foster a conducive environment for economic growth and social development.

Q.13. "Section 11-A of the Industrial Dispute Act, 1947 gives discretionary power to the Labour Court, Industrial Tribunal and National Tribunal to give appropriate relief to the discharged or dismissed workmen".

Comment.

Ans. Section 11-A of the Industrial Disputes Act, 1947, grants discretionary power to the Labour Court, Industrial Tribunal, and National Tribunal to provide appropriate relief to discharged or dismissed workmen. This provision empowers these tribunals to determine the validity of dismissals or discharge of employees and to order reinstatement with or without back wages, compensation, or any other relief they deem fit based on the facts and circumstances of each case.

The discretionary power conferred by Section 11-A allows the tribunals to consider various factors, including the nature of the misconduct, the length of service, the employee's past record, the employer's disciplinary policies, and the principles of natural justice, in making their decision. This flexibility enables the tribunals to render fair and just judgments tailored to the specific circumstances of each case, ensuring that the rights of both employers and employees are upheld.

However, this discretionary power also entails a level of judicial discretion, which may lead to varying interpretations and outcomes in different cases. While it provides tribunals with the necessary flexibility to deliver equitable justice, it also underscores the importance of exercising this discretion judiciously and impartially to promote fairness, uphold labor rights, and maintain industrial harmony.

2017 Question Paper

Q.1. Workman.

Ans. A "workman" is defined under Section 2(s) of the Industrial Disputes Act, 1947, as any individual (including apprentices) engaged in any industry to perform manual, unskilled, skilled, technical, operational, clerical, or supervisory tasks for compensation, whether explicitly stated in the employment terms or implied. This definition also encompasses individuals who have been terminated, discharged, or laid off due to or as a result of an industrial dispute, or whose termination, discharge, or layoff has triggered such a dispute.

However, the definition excludes individuals who fall under the following categories:

(i) Those who are subject to the Air Force Act, 1950, the Army Act, 1950, or the Navy Act, 1957.

(ii) Those employed in law enforcement or as officers or staff of a correctional facility.

(iii) Those primarily engaged in managerial or administrative roles.

(iv) Those employed in a supervisory capacity who receive wages exceeding ten thousand rupees per month or primarily perform managerial duties due to the nature of their position or the authority vested in them.

Case Law: The Supreme Court of India in the case of Bangalore Water Supply & Sewerage Board v. A. Rajappa (1978 AIR 548) emphasized that the determination of whether an individual qualifies as a "workman" under the Industrial Disputes Act depends on the nature of their duties and their relationship with the employer, regardless of their job title or designation.

Q.2. Work Committee.

Ans. Under Section 3 of the Industrial Disputes Act, provision is made for the establishment of a Works Committee in industrial establishments where one hundred or more workers are employed or have been employed within the preceding twelve months. The appropriate Government can mandate the formation of such a committee through general or specific orders. This committee comprises representatives from both the employers and the workers engaged in the establishment, ensuring that the number of worker representatives is not fewer than those of the employer. Worker representatives are selected from among the employees of the establishment, in consultation with their registered trade union, if any.

The Works Committee is entrusted with the responsibility of fostering harmony and positive relations between the employer and the employees. To fulfill this duty, the committee is required to address matters of mutual interest or concern and strive to resolve any significant differences of opinion on such matters.

Case Law: In the case of Bangalore Water Supply & Sewerage Board v. Rajappa (AIR 1978 SC 548), the Supreme Court of India highlighted the importance of Works Committees in promoting effective communication and resolving disputes at the workplace. The court emphasized that Works Committees serve as a platform for dialogue and cooperation between labor and management, ultimately contributing to the overall industrial peace and productivity.

Q.3. Appropriate Government.

Ans. As defined under Section 2(a) of the Industrial Disputes Act, 1947, the term "appropriate Government" holds significance in various contexts:

(i) For industrial disputes related to industries operated by or under the authority of the Central Government, including railway companies or specified controlled industries, or involving entities like Dock Labour Boards, the Industrial Finance Corporation of India Limited, the Employees' State Insurance Corporation, the Coal Mines Provident Fund Board, the Employees' Provident Fund Board, the Life Insurance Corporation of India, the Oil and Natural Gas Corporation Limited, the Deposit Insurance and Credit Guarantee Corporation, the Central Warehousing Corporation, the Unit Trust of India, the Food Corporation of India, the Airports Authority of India, Regional Rural Banks, the Export Credit and Guarantee Corporation Limited, the Industrial Reconstruction Bank of India, and the National Housing Bank, among others. Additionally, it extends to air transport services, banking or insurance companies, mines, oilfields, Cantonment Boards, major ports, companies with majority Central Government shareholding, and other corporations established by or under Parliament's law, as well as Central public sector undertakings, their subsidiary companies, and autonomous bodies under Central Government control.

(ii) For any other industrial dispute, including those involving State public sector undertakings, subsidiary companies, and autonomous bodies owned or controlled by the State Government, the appropriate Government is the State Government. However, in disputes between a contractor and contract labor employed through the contractor in an industrial establishment, the relevant Government is determined based on the authority controlling the industrial establishment in question.

Case Law: The case of Bangalore Water Supply & Sewerage Board v. A. Rajappa (AIR 1978 SC 548) underscores the significance of defining the "appropriate Government" in industrial disputes. It establishes that the determination of the appropriate Government plays a crucial role in the resolution and adjudication of disputes, ensuring effective governance and enforcement of labor laws at both the Central and State levels.

Q.4. Award

Ans. Sections 16, 17, and 17A of the Industrial Disputes Act outline the procedures and provisions regarding the form, publication, and commencement of reports and awards:

- **Form of report or award (Section 16) :**

1. Reports from Boards or Courts must be in writing and signed by all members. Members have the liberty to record any dissenting views.
2. Awards from Labor Courts, Tribunals, or National Tribunals are also required to be in writing and signed by the presiding officer.

- **Publication of reports and awards (Section 17):**

1. Reports from Boards or Courts, along with any recorded dissents, arbitration awards, and awards from Labor Courts, Tribunals, or National Tribunals, must be published by the appropriate Government within thirty days of receipt.
2. Once published, the award is deemed final and cannot be challenged in any court.

- **Commencement of the award: Section 17 A**

1. An award, including arbitration awards, becomes enforceable thirty days after publication under Section 17 A.
2. However, if the appropriate Government or the Central Government deems it detrimental to national economy or social justice to enforce the award, they can declare so through an official notification.
3. The Government then has ninety days from publication to reject or modify the award, and the decision is presented before the respective legislative bodies.
4. If the award is rejected or modified, it becomes enforceable fifteen days after being laid before the legislature.
5. If no action is taken within the ninety-day period, the award becomes enforceable.
6. The award comes into operation on the specified date within it or upon becoming enforceable.

Case Law: In the case of Indian Iron & Steel Co. Ltd. v. Their Workmen (AIR 1958 SC 130), the Supreme Court emphasized the importance of adhering to the statutory provisions regarding the form, publication, and commencement of awards under the Industrial Disputes Act. The court held that strict compliance with these provisions ensures transparency, fairness, and the effective resolution of industrial disputes.

Q.5. Collective Bargaining.

Ans. Collective bargaining is a process wherein representatives of employees, typically labor unions, negotiate with employers or their representatives to reach agreements on terms and conditions of employment. This negotiation encompasses various aspects such as wages, benefits, working hours, and working conditions. Through collective bargaining, both parties engage in dialogue, present their interests and concerns, and work towards reaching mutually acceptable agreements. Collective bargaining plays a crucial role in industrial relations, promoting cooperation, resolving conflicts, and ensuring the protection of workers' rights. It is a fundamental mechanism for achieving fair and equitable outcomes in the workplace while maintaining harmonious employer-employee relations.

Q.6. State the liabilities of a registered Trade Union.

Ans. A registered trade union assumes several liabilities, including legal obligations towards its members and adherence to statutory requirements. These liabilities typically include:

Duty of fair representation: The trade union must represent its members' interests fairly and without discrimination.

Compliance with labor laws: The union is responsible for ensuring compliance with relevant labor legislation, including filing statutory returns and maintaining financial records.

Financial accountability: The union must manage its finances responsibly, ensuring transparency and accountability in its financial transactions.

Liability for actions: The union may be held liable for the actions or decisions taken on behalf of its members, including any legal disputes or liabilities arising from collective actions or agreements.

Q.7. When a strike becomes illegal?

Ans. A strike becomes illegal when it violates the provisions of labor laws or specific regulations governing industrial action. This may occur if the strike is undertaken in contravention of procedures outlined in labor laws, such as failure to provide prior notice to the employer or appropriate authorities, or if it disrupts essential services or public order. Strikes can also be deemed illegal if they are declared by unions or employees engaged in prohibited or essential services, as defined by law. Additionally, any strike that involves violence, coercion, or intimidation may be considered illegal, undermining the principles of peaceful industrial action.

Q.8. When can an individual's dispute become an industrial dispute?

Ans. An individual's dispute can become an industrial dispute when it transcends the individual level and assumes collective significance that impacts the broader interests of workers or the functioning of an industry. Several factors can contribute to this transformation:

Collective action: If multiple employees raise similar grievances or concerns related to their employment terms, wages, working conditions, or rights, their individual disputes may coalesce into a collective dispute representing the broader workforce.

Union involvement: When a trade union intervenes to support an individual employee's grievance or organizes collective action on behalf of its members, the dispute may acquire an industrial character, reflecting the collective interests of the unionized workforce.

Impact on production: If an individual dispute disrupts or threatens to disrupt the normal functioning of an industry, causing production delays, loss of revenue, or affecting other workers' employment, it may be treated as an industrial dispute.

An individual's dispute evolves into an industrial dispute when it assumes collective significance, impacts the broader workforce or industry, and requires intervention at a systemic level to resolve effectively.

Q.9. Discuss the procedure for the registration of a Trade Union. How many members are required for the registration of a Trade Union?

Ans. The procedure for the registration of a trade union in India is governed by the Trade Unions Act, 1926. To register a trade union, the following steps must be followed:

Application: The trade union must submit an application to the Registrar of Trade Unions in the state where the union's head office is located. The application must be signed by at least seven members who are eligible for membership under the Act.

Memorandum: The application must be accompanied by a memorandum of association of the trade union containing details such as the name, objectives, and rules of the union.

Rules: The trade union must also submit a copy of its rules, which outline the procedures for membership, meetings, elections, and other organizational matters.

Registration: Upon receipt of the application and documents, the Registrar will scrutinize the same and, if satisfied, register the trade union. Once registered, the union becomes a legal entity with certain rights and obligations.

As per the Trade Unions Act, 1926, a trade union must have a minimum of seven members to be eligible for registration. These members must be workers employed in industries specified in the Act, such as manufacturing, mining, or transport. The Act also specifies that the members must pay a subscription fee to the union for a specified period to demonstrate their commitment to the organization.

Q.10. Who are disqualified to be office bearer of a registered Trade Union? Can a minor be a member of a registered trade union?

Ans. Under the Trade Unions Act, 1926, certain individuals are disqualified from holding office bearer positions in a registered trade union. These include:

Minors: Persons who have not attained the age of eighteen years are disqualified from being office bearers of a registered trade union.

Non-citizens: Individuals who are not citizens of India are disqualified from holding office in a registered trade union.

Insolvents: Persons who have been declared insolvent and whose insolvency has not been discharged are disqualified from holding office.

Persons convicted of certain offenses: Individuals who have been convicted of offenses involving moral turpitude or offenses related to breach of trust, unless a period of five years has elapsed since their release, are disqualified.

Persons dismissed or removed from employment: Individuals who have been dismissed or removed from employment for misconduct and have not been reinstated or re-employed are disqualified.

Regarding the membership of minors in a registered trade union, while there is no explicit prohibition under the Trade Unions Act, 1926, it is generally understood that minors cannot enter into contracts or participate in legal proceedings independently. Therefore, minors may not be able to fully exercise their rights as trade union members or participate in union activities effectively. However, they may still be associated with the union as non-office-bearing members, depending on the union's rules and policies.

Q.11. "Lock out is a weapon in the hands of employers and strike, in the hands of workers." Discuss under the provisions of Industrial Dispute Act, 1947.

Ans. The Industrial Disputes Act, 1947, provides for both lockouts by employers and strikes by workers as legitimate instruments to resolve labor disputes. A lockout refers to the temporary closure or suspension of work by an employer as a preemptive measure during an industrial dispute, intended to pressure workers or their union to accept the employer's terms. Section 22 of the Act outlines the conditions under which a lockout may be declared, including the provision of notice to the appropriate government authority and affected workers.

Similarly, Section 22 of the Act recognizes the right of workers to strike as a means of protesting against unfair labor practices or pressing for their demands. Strikes may be declared after giving notice to the employer and fulfilling other statutory requirements specified under the Act.

Both lockouts and strikes can disrupt production, cause economic losses, and escalate tensions between employers and employees. However, they serve as bargaining tools that compel parties to engage in negotiations and find amicable solutions to their disputes. The Industrial Disputes Act, 1947, seeks to regulate the use of these instruments to ensure they are employed judiciously and in accordance with the principles of fairness, industrial peace, and social justice, thereby maintaining a balance of power between employers and workers.

Q.12. Define and discuss in detail "Industrial Dispute" under the Industrial Dispute Act, 1947.

Ans. An "industrial dispute" under the Industrial Disputes Act, 1947, refers to any disagreement or conflict between employers and employees, or between employees themselves, arising during the course of employment. This conflict may pertain to various aspects of employment, including wages, benefits, working conditions, disciplinary actions, or the interpretation of service conditions.

The Act defines industrial disputes broadly, covering disputes between employers and workmen, workmen and workmen, or between employers' associations and workmen's associations. It encompasses disputes of both individual and collective nature, representing the interests of workers as a group rather than on an individual basis.

Industrial disputes can manifest in different forms, such as strikes, lockouts, protests, or grievances raised through formal channels. These disputes often arise due to perceived injustices, unequal treatment, or unmet expectations among the workforce, leading to tensions between labor and management.

The Industrial Disputes Act, 1947, provides a comprehensive framework for the prevention and resolution of industrial disputes. It outlines procedures for conciliation, arbitration, and adjudication by labor courts or tribunals to facilitate the amicable settlement of disputes and promote industrial peace. The Act also defines the roles and responsibilities of employers, employees, and government authorities in managing industrial disputes, ensuring fair treatment, protecting workers' rights, and maintaining harmonious industrial relations.

Q. 13. Discuss procedure, powers and functions of National Industrial Tribunal under Industrial Dispute Act, 1947.

Ans. The National Industrial Tribunal (NIT) is a specialized adjudicatory body established under the Industrial Disputes Act, 1947, to adjudicate industrial disputes of national significance. Its primary function is to provide a forum for the resolution of complex and critical industrial disputes that impact national interests or involve multiple states or industries.

The procedure for adjudication by the National Industrial Tribunal involves the submission of disputes to the Central Government, which then refers them to the Tribunal for adjudication. The Tribunal conducts hearings, examines evidence, and makes decisions on the disputes referred to it by the Government.

The National Industrial Tribunal possesses extensive powers to conduct proceedings, summon witnesses, examine evidence, and issue orders or awards to resolve disputes. Its decisions are final and binding on the parties involved, subject to limited avenues of appeal.

The functions of the National Industrial Tribunal encompass not only the resolution of disputes but also the promotion of industrial peace and harmony. It aims to strike a balance between the interests of employers and employees, uphold labor rights, and foster a conducive environment for economic growth and social development.

The National Industrial Tribunal plays a vital role in adjudicating complex industrial disputes of national significance, ensuring timely and effective resolution while safeguarding the interests of all stakeholders involved.

CHAPTER THREE

Environmental Law

Environment Law 2023 Question Paper

Q.1. Sustainable Development and Environment.

Ans. Sustainable development balances economic growth, social inclusion, and environmental protection for long-term well-being. It emphasizes efficient resource use, reduced pollution, and conservation of biodiversity. By integrating sustainability into development, societies can achieve prosperity while preserving the planet for future generations.

Q.2. Greenhouse effect.

Ans. The greenhouse effect is a natural process where certain gases in the atmosphere trap heat from the sun, warming the Earth. This process is essential for life, but human activities have increased greenhouse gas concentrations, intensifying warming and contributing to climate change.

Q.3. Fundamental duties concerning environment under constitution of India.

Ans. The Constitution of India outlines fundamental duties concerning the environment in Article 51A(g). This duty obligates citizens to protect and improve the natural environment, including forests, lakes, rivers, and wildlife, and to have compassion for living creatures. By promoting environmental conservation and ethical stewardship, citizens contribute to sustainable development and the preservation of India's natural heritage for future generations.

Q.4. 'Environment is everything which is not me.' Explain briefly.

Ans. The statement "Environment is everything which is not me" refers to the idea that the environment encompasses all external factors and elements that surround an individual. This includes natural features such as air, water, soil, plants, and animals, as well as human-made structures and social constructs like cities, buildings, and communities. Essentially, the environment is the broader context in which a person exists, impacting their life and experiences while being separate from their own identity and actions.

Q.5. 'Air Polluter' under the Air (Prevention and Control of Pollution) Act, 1981.

Ans. An "air polluter" under the Air (Prevention and Control of Pollution) Act, 1981, is any person, agency, or industry responsible for releasing air pollutants that exceed the permissible limits set by the Act. This includes emissions from vehicles, factories, power plants, construction activities, and other sources that contaminate the atmosphere. The Act empowers state pollution control boards to monitor and regulate air quality, as well as take action against air polluters to protect public health and the environment from the harmful effects of air pollution.

Q.6. Explain environemnt protection and ancient Indian philosophy relating to environment protection.

Ans. Ancient Indian philosophy emphasizes harmony between humans and nature, rooted in the belief that the natural world is sacred and interconnected. Texts like the Vedas, Upanishads, and Puranas advocate respect for all living beings and sustainable living practices. Concepts such as Ahimsa (non-violence) and Prakriti (nature) highlight the importance of preserving the environment. Ancient rituals and customs, such as worshiping rivers and trees, also underscore the reverence for nature. These philosophies align with modern concepts of environmental protection, advocating for stewardship and conservation of natural resources for future generations.

Q.7. Examine the scope of section 133 of code of criminal procedure as a tool for combating environmental pollution.

Ans. Section 133 of the Code of Criminal Procedure (CrPC) serves as a tool for combating environmental pollution by addressing public nuisances that threaten public health and safety. This section empowers a magistrate to issue orders to remove or stop any activity that pollutes air, water, or land. It covers a wide range of nuisances, including hazardous emissions, water contamination, and improper waste disposal. Non-compliance can result in penalties, ensuring swift action against polluters. Thus, Section 133 plays a crucial role in preventing and mitigating environmental pollution through legal enforcement and accountability.

Q.8. Discuss the constitution of State Board under Water (Prevention and Control of Pollution), Act, 1974.

Ans. Under the Water (Prevention and Control of Pollution) Act, 1974, each state is required to establish a State Pollution Control Board. The constitution of the State Board is governed by Section 4 of the Act. The State Board consists of a chairman and members nominated by the state government. These members include representatives from local authorities, industry, agriculture, fisheries, and the scientific community, as well as individuals with experience in water pollution control. The Board is tasked with overseeing water quality, monitoring pollution levels, and implementing regulatory measures to prevent and control water pollution within the state.

Q.9. What is called environmental pollution? What are its different kinds? What is its global effect?

Ans. Environment pollution refers to the introduction of harmful substances or pollutants into the natural environment, resulting in adverse effects on ecosystems, human health, and the quality of life. These pollutants can originate from natural or human-made sources and disrupt the ecological balance of air, water, and land.

Types of Environment Pollution:

Air Pollution: The presence of harmful gasses, particulates, or biological molecules in the atmosphere. Sources include industrial emissions, vehicle exhaust, and the burning of fossil fuels.

Water Pollution: Contamination of water bodies such as rivers, lakes, oceans, and groundwater. Sources include industrial discharge, agricultural runoff, sewage, and oil spills.

Land Pollution: The degradation of the earth's surface due to improper disposal of waste, industrial activity, and deforestation. It includes soil contamination and loss of arable land.

Noise Pollution: Excessive or disturbing levels of noise from sources such as traffic, construction, and industrial activities, affecting human and animal health.

Light Pollution: Excessive or misdirected artificial light that disrupts natural cycles and impacts wildlife and human health.

Thermal Pollution: The release of heat into the environment, primarily from power plants and industrial processes, impacting aquatic and terrestrial ecosystems.

Global Effects:

Climate Change: Greenhouse gas emissions lead to global warming, causing shifts in weather patterns, melting glaciers, and rising sea levels.

Loss of Biodiversity: Pollution disrupts habitats, leading to species extinction and loss of ecosystem services.

Human Health Impacts: Pollution causes respiratory diseases, cancers, and other health issues.

Water Scarcity: Contamination of water sources reduces the availability of clean drinking water.

Ozone Layer Depletion: Certain pollutants, such as chlorofluorocarbons (CFCs), damage the ozone layer, increasing UV radiation exposure.

Economic Costs: Environmental pollution leads to economic losses through healthcare costs, reduced productivity, and damage to agriculture and fisheries.

Environment pollution encompasses various types of contaminants that harm ecosystems, human health, and the planet. Its global effects are far-reaching, requiring concerted international efforts to mitigate and manage pollution for a sustainable future.

Q.10. Is protection of the environment a fundamental right? Explain with the help of relevant provisions and case law.

Ans. Yes, the protection of the environment has been recognized as a fundamental right under the Constitution of India. Although the Constitution does not explicitly mention the right to a clean environment, the Supreme Court of India has interpreted the right to life and personal liberty (Article 21) to include the right to a healthy and clean environment.

Relevant Provisions:

Article 21 - Right to Life: The Supreme Court of India has interpreted the right to life to include the right to a healthy environment as an integral part of the right to live with dignity and well-being.

Article 48A - Protection and Improvement of Environment: This directive principle of state policy mandates that the state shall endeavor to protect and improve the environment and to safeguard the forests and wildlife of the country.

Article 51A(g) - Fundamental Duties: This article imposes a duty on every citizen to protect and improve the natural environment, including forests, lakes, rivers, and wildlife, and to have compassion for living creatures.

Case Law:

M.C. Mehta v. Union of India (1986): The Supreme Court held that the right to life under Article 21 includes the right to a healthy environment. In this case, the court ordered the closure of polluting industries around the Taj Mahal to protect the monument and the environment.

Subhash Kumar v. State of Bihar (1991): The court recognized the right to a pollution-free water and air as part of the right to life under Article 21.

Vellore Citizens' Welfare Forum v. Union of India (1996): This landmark case emphasized the importance of sustainable development and the need to balance industrial growth with environmental protection. The court recognized the precautionary principle and the polluter-pays principle as part of Indian law.

These cases illustrate how the Indian judiciary has interpreted Article 21 to encompass the right to a clean and healthy environment, thereby making environmental protection a fundamental right. This interpretation serves as a basis for judicial intervention and policy-making to safeguard the environment and public health.

Q.11. What are the restrictions on use of industrial plants under Air (prevention and control of pollution) Act, 1981.

Ans. The Air (Prevention and Control of Pollution) Act, 1981, is a comprehensive legislation in India aimed at preventing, controlling, and reducing air pollution from industrial plants and other sources. The Act provides various restrictions on the use of industrial plants to ensure air quality and protect the environment. These restrictions are implemented through state pollution control boards and include the following key provisions:

Consent Requirement: Industrial plants must obtain consent from the State Pollution Control Board (SPCB) to establish or operate any plant that may cause air pollution. This consent specifies the emissions limits and other conditions that the plant must adhere to.

Emission Standards: The Act authorizes SPCBs to set emission standards for industrial plants based on the type of industry, location, and other factors. These standards limit the concentration and types of pollutants that can be released into the atmosphere.

Monitoring and Inspections: Industrial plants are subject to regular monitoring and inspections by SPCBs to ensure compliance with emission standards and other regulatory requirements. Plants must allow access to SPCB officials for inspections.

Installation of Pollution Control Equipment: Industrial plants are required to install and maintain appropriate pollution control equipment to minimize emissions. This may include filters, scrubbers, and other devices designed to reduce air pollutants.

Prohibition on Certain Activities: The Act may prohibit specific activities or emissions that are deemed hazardous to public health or the environment. For example, certain industrial processes that release toxic gasses may be restricted.

Compliance with Directions: SPCBs can issue directions to industrial plants to take corrective measures, including discontinuing operations, reducing emissions, or installing new pollution control technology.

Legal Consequences for Non-Compliance: Failure to comply with the Act's provisions, including obtaining consent or adhering to emission standards, can result in penalties, fines, or closure of the plant. Legal action may be taken against industrial plants that violate the Act.

The Air (Prevention and Control of Pollution) Act, 1981, imposes various restrictions on industrial plants to control air pollution and protect public health and the environment. Compliance with these restrictions is essential for sustainable industrial development and the well-being of communities.

Q.12. What is the National Green Tribunal? How is it constituted? What are its powers and functions? Explain with decided cases.

Ans. The National Green Tribunal (NGT) is a specialized legal body in India established under the National Green Tribunal Act, 2010. It is tasked with the effective and expeditious disposal of cases related to environmental protection, conservation of forests, and other natural resources, including enforcement of any legal rights relating to the environment.

Constitution:

The NGT consists of a chairperson, who must be a retired Supreme Court judge, and other judicial and expert members. The members are appointed by the central government based on their qualifications and expertise in legal and environmental matters. The Tribunal has benches located in different parts of India, with its principal bench in New Delhi.

Powers and Functions:

Adjudication and Resolution: The NGT hears and resolves disputes and claims related to environmental protection, conservation of forests, and other natural resources.

Enforcement of Legal Rights: It enforces legal rights concerning the environment, including taking actions to prevent, control, and reverse environmental damage.

Suo Motu Powers: The Tribunal can take suo motu (on its own motion) cognizance of environmental issues and take necessary action.

Penalties and Compensation: The NGT can impose penalties and order compensation for damages caused by environmental violations.

Appeals: The NGT hears appeals against decisions of state pollution control boards and other authorities related to environmental issues.

Decided Cases:

Sterlite Copper Case (2019): The NGT ordered the closure of the Sterlite Copper plant in Tuticorin, Tamil Nadu, due to serious environmental violations and impact on the health of nearby residents.

Yamuna River Pollution Case (2015): The NGT passed several orders to clean up the Yamuna River and held various industries accountable for discharging untreated waste into the river.

Delhi Air Pollution Case (2016): The NGT imposed restrictions on construction activities, burning of waste, and vehicular emissions in Delhi to combat severe air pollution.

These decided cases demonstrate the NGT's role in safeguarding the environment by taking decisive actions against polluters and enforcing environmental laws effectively. Through its powers and functions, the NGT plays a crucial role in promoting sustainable development and environmental justice in India.

Q.13. Write a short not on any of the following:

Polluter Pay Principle

Ans. The polluter pays principle (PPP) is a fundamental environmental policy concept that assigns responsibility for environmental damage to those who cause it. It stipulates that polluters should bear the costs of remedying or mitigating the pollution they generate, rather than shifting the burden onto society or the environment. The PPP aims to internalize the external costs of pollution by incentivizing polluters to adopt cleaner production methods, reduce emissions, and invest in pollution control technologies. By holding polluters accountable for their actions, the PPP encourages environmental stewardship, economic efficiency, and sustainable development. This principle is enshrined in various international agreements, national environmental laws, and regulatory frameworks as a guiding principle for environmental governance, emphasizing the importance of environmental responsibility and accountability in safeguarding our planet's health and well-being.

Public Trust Doctrine

Ans. The public trust doctrine is a legal principle that holds certain natural resources in trust for the benefit of the public. Originating from Roman law and later affirmed in common law, it asserts that certain resources, such as navigable waters, beaches, and the atmosphere, are held by the government as trustees for the use and enjoyment of present and future generations. The doctrine imposes a duty on the government to protect and preserve these resources for public use, prohibiting their privatization or depletion for private gain. It also grants citizens the right to challenge government actions that threaten the integrity of public trust resources. The public trust doctrine serves as a cornerstone of environmental law, ensuring equitable access to essential resources and promoting sustainable management for the collective well-being of society.

Current Environmental Problems.

Ans. Current environmental problems pose significant challenges to ecosystems, biodiversity, and human health worldwide. These issues include climate change, deforestation, air and water pollution, loss of biodiversity, and plastic pollution. Climate change, driven by greenhouse gas emissions from human activities, is causing rising temperatures, extreme weather events, and sea-level rise, threatening vulnerable communities and ecosystems. Deforestation contributes to habitat loss, soil erosion, and loss of biodiversity, exacerbating climate change and reducing carbon sequestration capacity. Air and water pollution from industrial activities, transportation, and agriculture pose risks to human health and ecosystems, leading to respiratory diseases, contaminated water sources, and ecosystem degradation. Loss of biodiversity due to habitat destruction, overexploitation of resources, and invasive species threatens the stability of ecosystems and the services they provide. Plastic pollution, particularly in oceans, harms marine life, disrupts ecosystems, and contaminates food webs. Addressing these environmental problems requires urgent global action, collaboration, and innovative solutions to ensure a sustainable future for all.

Environment law 2022 Question Paper

Q.1. Environment Laboratories.

Ans. Environmental laboratories are specialized facilities equipped to analyze and assess various environmental parameters, such as air quality, water quality, soil composition, and biological contaminants. These laboratories employ advanced techniques and instruments to detect pollutants, monitor environmental trends, and ensure compliance with regulatory standards. Environmental laboratories play a crucial role in environmental monitoring, research, and risk assessment, providing valuable data and insights to government agencies, industries, and research institutions. They contribute to environmental protection efforts by identifying sources of pollution, evaluating the effectiveness of mitigation measures, and supporting evidence-based decision-making for sustainable resource management and conservation.

Q.2. Protected Forests.

Ans. Protected forests refer to designated areas of land that are legally protected and managed to conserve biodiversity, preserve natural habitats, and sustain ecosystem services. These forests may include national parks, wildlife sanctuaries, biosphere reserves, and conservation areas established under environmental laws and regulations. Protected forests serve as havens for endangered species, maintain ecological balance, and provide recreational and educational opportunities for visitors. They play a vital role in mitigating climate change, enhancing carbon sequestration, and safeguarding genetic diversity. Effective management and enforcement measures are essential to ensure the long-term conservation and integrity of protected forests for future generations.

Q.3. Hazardous Substances.

Ans. Hazardous substances are materials that pose a risk to human health, the environment, or property due to their chemical, physical, or biological properties. These substances include toxic chemicals, radioactive materials, flammable liquids, corrosive agents, and infectious pathogens. Exposure to hazardous substances can lead to acute or chronic health effects, such as poisoning, respiratory ailments, cancer, or reproductive disorders. Improper handling, storage, or disposal of hazardous substances can result in environmental contamination, soil and water pollution, and ecological harm. Regulatory frameworks, safety protocols, and risk management practices are implemented to minimize the risks associated with hazardous substances and protect public health and the environment.

Q.4. Define Pollution.

Ans. Pollution refers to the introduction of harmful or unwanted substances or contaminants into the environment, causing adverse effects on ecosystems, human health, and the quality of life. These pollutants can originate from various sources, including industrial activities, transportation, agriculture, and waste disposal. Common types of pollution include air pollution (emission of gases and particulates), water pollution (contamination of water bodies), soil pollution (degradation of soil quality), noise pollution (excessive or disruptive noise), and light pollution (excessive artificial light). Pollution poses significant environmental, social, and economic challenges, necessitating measures to mitigate its impacts and promote sustainable development.

Q.5. What is the purpose of the constitution of an area as a National Park?

Ans. The purpose of designating an area as a National Park is to preserve and protect its natural beauty, ecological integrity, and biodiversity for future generations. National Parks serve as sanctuaries for diverse plant and animal species, providing habitats for wildlife to thrive and ecosystems to flourish. They offer opportunities for recreation, education, and scientific research while promoting environmental awareness and stewardship. By safeguarding these areas from development, exploitation, and human disturbance, National Parks contribute to the conservation of natural resources, the promotion of sustainable tourism, and the enhancement of the overall quality of life.

Q.6. Discuss ancient Indian philosophy relating to the Protection of environment.

Ans. Ancient Indian philosophy reflects a deep reverence and respect for the environment, rooted in the belief that nature is sacred and interconnected with human life. The principles of Ahimsa (non-violence) and Dharma (righteousness) underscored the importance of living in harmony with all living beings and the natural world. Texts such as the Vedas, Upanishads, and Puranas emphasized the interconnectedness of all life forms and advocated for the preservation and protection of the environment. Practices such as tree worship, river reverence, and conservation of natural resources were integral parts of ancient Indian culture. Additionally, concepts like Prakriti (nature) and Vasudhaiva Kutumbakam (the world is one family) emphasized the interconnectedness of all living beings and the responsibility to care for the environment. These philosophical teachings continue to inspire environmental conservation efforts in modern India, highlighting the enduring relevance of ancient wisdom in promoting ecological harmony and sustainability.

Q.7. Discuss different kinds of Pollution.

Ans. Pollution manifests in various forms, each with distinct impacts on the environment, human health, and ecosystems. The main types of pollution include:

Air Pollution: Caused by the release of harmful gasses, particulate matter, and pollutants into the atmosphere from sources such as industrial emissions, vehicle exhaust, and agricultural activities. Air pollution leads to respiratory illnesses, cardiovascular diseases, and environmental degradation.

Water Pollution: Occurs when contaminants, including chemicals, pathogens, and waste, enter water bodies such as rivers, lakes, and oceans. Sources of water pollution include industrial discharge, agricultural runoff, sewage, and oil spills. Water pollution affects aquatic ecosystems, compromises water quality, and poses risks to human health.

Soil Pollution: Results from the accumulation of hazardous substances, heavy metals, pesticides, and industrial waste in the soil. Soil pollution degrades soil fertility, affects crop yields, and contaminates groundwater, leading to ecological imbalance and food safety concerns.

Noise Pollution: Arises from excessive or disruptive noise from sources such as traffic, construction, industrial activities, and urbanization. Noise pollution disturbs wildlife, causes stress and hearing loss in humans, and disrupts communication and sleep patterns.

Light Pollution: Caused by excessive or misdirected artificial light, which interferes with natural light cycles, disrupts ecosystems, and affects wildlife behavior, migration, and reproduction.

Plastic Pollution: Results from the accumulation of plastic waste in the environment, particularly in oceans and waterways. Plastic pollution harms marine life, contaminates food chains, and degrades ecosystems, posing significant environmental and health risks.

These different forms of pollution highlight the complex and interconnected nature of environmental degradation and underscore the urgent need for comprehensive mitigation and management strategies to address these challenges.

Q.8. Ozone layer Depletion is causing Damage to the environment. Comment.

Ans. Ozone layer depletion is a significant environmental concern with far-reaching consequences for the planet. The ozone layer, located in the Earth's stratosphere, plays a crucial role in protecting life on Earth by absorbing harmful ultraviolet (UV) radiation from the sun. However, the release of ozone-depleting substances (ODS), such as chlorofluorocarbons (CFCs), halons, and methyl bromide, has led to the thinning of the ozone layer, particularly over polar regions.

The consequences of ozone layer depletion are profound and multifaceted. Increased UV radiation reaching the Earth's surface poses serious risks to human health, including an elevated risk of skin cancer, cataracts, and immune system suppression. UV radiation also harms terrestrial and aquatic ecosystems, damaging phytoplankton, corals, and plants, disrupting food chains, and reducing biodiversity.

Ozone depletion exacerbates climate change by altering atmospheric circulation patterns and contributing to global warming. Changes in temperature and weather patterns impact agriculture, water resources, and weather-related disasters, posing additional challenges for human societies and ecosystems.

Addressing ozone layer depletion requires international cooperation and concerted efforts to phase out ozone-depleting substances, as demonstrated by the Montreal Protocol, a landmark international treaty aimed at protecting the ozone layer. While significant progress has been made in reducing ODS emissions, continued vigilance and action are essential to safeguard the ozone layer and mitigate its adverse impacts on the environment, human health, and global climate.

Q.9. Explain the constitution, powers and functions of the National Green Tribunal.

Ans. The National Green Tribunal (NGT) is a specialized judicial body established in India under the National Green Tribunal Act, 2010, to address environmental disputes and promote environmental justice. The NGT consists of both judicial and expert members and has jurisdiction over matters related to environmental protection, conservation of natural resources, and enforcement of environmental laws.

Constitution: The NGT comprises a chairperson, who must be a retired judge of the Supreme Court, and other judicial and expert members appointed by the central government. The Tribunal has regional benches located across India to ensure accessibility to justice.

Powers and Functions:

Adjudication: The NGT hears and adjudicates cases related to environmental protection, conservation, and management, including disputes between parties regarding environmental laws and regulations.

Enforcement: The NGT has the power to enforce its orders and directions, ensuring compliance with environmental laws and regulations.

Suo Motu Action: The NGT can take suo motu cognizance of matters related to environmental protection and conservation and initiate legal proceedings accordingly.

Appeals: Parties aggrieved by the decisions of environmental regulatory authorities or tribunals can appeal to the NGT for redressal.

Expertise: The NGT includes expert members with knowledge and experience in environmental science, engineering, and law, ensuring informed decision-making on environmental matters.

Penalties and Compensation: The NGT can impose penalties, fines, or compensation orders on individuals, industries, or authorities responsible for environmental violations.

Overall, the NGT plays a crucial role in promoting environmental justice, ensuring effective enforcement of environmental laws, and advancing sustainable development in India. Its specialized expertise and powers contribute to the protection and conservation of the environment for present and future generations.

Q.10. Discuss the provisions under the constitution relating to the protection of the environment.

Ans. The Constitution of India contains several provisions that emphasize the importance of environmental protection and conservation. These provisions serve as the foundation for environmental governance and guide the formulation and implementation of environmental policies and laws in the country. Some key provisions include:

Article 48A - Protection and Improvement of Environment: This directive principle of state policy mandates that the state shall endeavor to protect and improve the environment and to safeguard the forests and wildlife of the country. It highlights the duty of the state to promote environmental sustainability and conservation efforts.

Article 51A(g) - Fundamental Duties: This article imposes a fundamental duty on every citizen to protect and improve the natural environment, including forests, lakes, rivers, and wildlife, and to have compassion for living creatures. It emphasizes the role of individuals in environmental stewardship and sustainable development.

Article 21 - Right to Life: The Supreme Court has interpreted the right to life under Article 21 to include the right to a healthy environment as an integral part of the right to live with dignity and well-being. This interpretation underscores the importance of environmental protection for ensuring fundamental human rights.

Article 253 - Power of Parliament to enact laws for implementing international agreements: This article empowers the Parliament to enact laws for implementing international agreements, including those related to environmental protection and conservation. It facilitates the adoption of international best practices and standards in environmental governance.

The constitutional provisions reflect India's commitment to environmental sustainability, conservation of natural resources, and the promotion of a healthy environment for present and future generations. They provide a framework for environmental governance and guide the development of policies and laws aimed at addressing environmental challenges and promoting sustainable development.

Q.11. Differentiate between reserve and protected forest? Discuss the rules laid down by the state Government to regulate matter and protect forests?

Ans. Reserve forests and protected forests are both categories of forests designated for conservation and protection, but they differ in their legal status, management objectives, and levels of human intervention.

Reserve Forests:

Legal Status: Reserve forests are declared as such under the Indian Forest Act, 1927. They are under the control and management of the state government.

Management Objectives: The primary objective of reserve forests is to conserve biodiversity, protect watersheds, and regulate forest activities for sustainable use. These forests have stricter regulations on human activities such as grazing, logging, and cultivation.

Human Intervention: Reserve forests are subject to limited human intervention, with controlled access and activities allowed only under permit from forest authorities.

Protected Forests:

Legal Status: Protected forests are also declared under the Indian Forest Act, 1927. They are managed by the state government for the purpose of preserving flora, fauna, and wildlife.

Management Objectives: Protected forests aim to conserve biodiversity, provide habitat for wildlife, and promote ecological balance. They may allow for some sustainable use and regulated human activities.

Human Intervention: Protected forests may permit certain activities such as sustainable harvesting of non-timber forest products, controlled grazing, and ecotourism, under strict regulations and supervision.

Rules Laid Down by State Governments:

State governments formulate rules and regulations to regulate and protect forests within their jurisdiction. These rules may include:

Forest Conservation Acts: Laws prohibiting unauthorized felling of trees, conversion of forests for non-forest purposes, and encroachment on forest land.

Forest Management Plans: Strategies for sustainable forest management, biodiversity conservation, and watershed protection.

Forest Protection Committees: Committees comprising local stakeholders to monitor and prevent illegal activities such as poaching, logging, and encroachment.

Permitting Systems: Procedures for obtaining permits or licenses for regulated activities such as timber harvesting, grazing, and tourism.

Ecotourism Guidelines: Guidelines for promoting responsible and sustainable ecotourism activities within forest areas while minimizing environmental impacts.

These rules and regulations are essential for ensuring the effective conservation and sustainable management of forest resources while balancing the needs of local communities and promoting biodiversity conservation.

Q.12. Discuss the provisions under Criminal Procedure Code 1975 for combating environmental pollution.

Ans. The Criminal Procedure Code, 1973 (CrPC) provides certain provisions to combat environmental pollution and address environmental offenses. These provisions empower law enforcement agencies and the judiciary to take action against individuals or entities responsible for polluting the environment. Some key provisions include:

Section 133 - Conditional Order for Removal of Nuisance: Under this section, a magistrate can issue a conditional order to remove or abate a nuisance that causes environmental pollution. This provision enables authorities to take swift action to address pollution issues and safeguard public health and the environment.

Section 268 - Public Nuisance: Section 268 of the CrPC deals with public nuisance offenses, which include acts that cause annoyance or injury to the public or pose a threat to public health or safety. Actions such as polluting water sources, emitting noxious fumes, or creating excessive noise may be considered public nuisances under this section.

Section 278 - Making atmosphere noxious to health: This section prohibits the emission of any noxious substance into the atmosphere, which is likely to cause injury to human health or impair the environment. Violation of this provision constitutes a criminal offense punishable under the law.

Section 430 - Mischief by injury to public road, bridge, river or channel: Section 430 of the CrPC deals with offenses related to causing damage or mischief to public property, including natural resources such as rivers, bridges, and channels. Actions that result in environmental damage or pollution may be prosecuted under this section.

Section 431 - Mischief by injury to public road, bridge, river or channel: Similar to Section 430, this section deals with offenses of causing damage or mischief to public property, including natural resources. Individuals or entities responsible for environmental pollution or degradation may be charged under this provision.

These provisions under the Criminal Procedure Code empower law enforcement authorities and the judiciary to take action against environmental offenders and protect the environment from pollution and degradation. They play a crucial role in enforcing environmental laws and regulations and ensuring accountability for actions that harm the environment.

Q.13. Discuss the provisions regarding the constitution, powers and functions of State Board under the Air (Prevention & Control, Pollution) Act 1981.

Ans. The Air (Prevention and Control of Pollution) Act, 1981, mandates the establishment of State Pollution Control Boards (SPCBs) to prevent and control air pollution in respective states. These boards play a crucial role in implementing air quality management strategies and enforcing regulatory measures to protect public health and the environment. Here are the provisions regarding the constitution, powers, and functions of SPCBs under the Act:

Constitution:

Composition: Each SPCB is composed of a chairperson, member-secretary, and other members appointed by the state government. The board includes experts in environmental science, pollution control, and related fields.

Qualifications: Members of the SPCB are appointed based on their expertise and experience in environmental management, science, engineering, or law.

Powers:

Regulatory Authority: SPCBs have the authority to enforce air quality standards, regulate industrial emissions, and monitor ambient air quality in their respective states.

Issuance of Directions: The boards can issue directives to industries, commercial establishments, and other polluting entities to comply with emission standards, adopt pollution control measures, and mitigate environmental pollution.

Inspection and Monitoring: SPCBs conduct regular inspections, surveys, and monitoring of air pollution sources, industrial units, and ambient air quality to assess compliance with regulatory standards.

Enforcement Actions: SPCBs have the power to initiate legal proceedings, impose penalties, and prosecute offenders for violations of air pollution control laws and regulations.

Research and Development: The boards facilitate research and development activities related to air pollution control technologies, best practices, and strategies to improve air quality.

Functions:

Air Quality Management: SPCBs formulate and implement air quality management plans, including the identification of pollution sources, establishment of emission standards, and development of pollution control strategies.

Public Awareness: The boards conduct awareness programs, seminars, and workshops to educate the public about the adverse effects of air pollution and promote pollution prevention and control measures.

Coordination: SPCBs collaborate with other government agencies, industries, non-governmental organizations, and stakeholders to address air pollution issues comprehensively and develop collaborative solutions.

Overall, State Pollution Control Boards play a crucial role in safeguarding air quality, promoting environmental sustainability, and protecting public health through effective pollution control measures and regulatory enforcement.

Environmental Law 2019 Question Paper

Q.1. What are the duties of a wildlife advisory board?

Ans. The Wildlife Advisory Board is tasked with advising the government on matters related to wildlife conservation and management. Its duties include:

Providing recommendations on the protection and conservation of wildlife species and habitats.

Advising on the establishment and management of protected areas, wildlife sanctuaries, and national parks.

Formulating policies and strategies for wildlife conservation and sustainable management.

Reviewing and assessing wildlife management plans and projects.

Recommending measures for mitigating human-wildlife conflicts and promoting coexistence.

Facilitating stakeholder engagement and collaboration in wildlife conservation efforts.

Overall, the Wildlife Advisory Board plays a crucial role in guiding wildlife conservation policies and initiatives to ensure the protection and sustainable management of wildlife resources.

Q.2. Protected forests.

Ans. Protected forests are designated areas of land that are legally protected and managed to conserve biodiversity, preserve natural habitats, and sustain ecosystem services. These forests may include national parks, wildlife sanctuaries, biosphere reserves, and conservation areas established under environmental laws and regulations. Protected forests serve as havens for endangered species, maintain ecological balance, and provide opportunities for recreation, research, and education. By safeguarding these areas from development, exploitation, and human disturbance, protected forests contribute to the conservation of natural resources, promotion of biodiversity, and enhancement of environmental quality for present and future generations.

Q.3. Hazardous substances.

Ans. Hazardous substances are materials that pose a risk to human health, the environment, or property due to their chemical, physical, or biological properties. These substances include toxic chemicals, radioactive materials, flammable liquids, corrosive agents, and infectious pathogens. Exposure to hazardous substances can lead to acute or chronic health effects, such as poisoning, respiratory ailments, cancer, or reproductive disorders. Improper handling, storage, or disposal of hazardous substances can result in environmental contamination, soil and water pollution, and ecological harm. Regulatory frameworks, safety protocols, and risk management practices are implemented to minimize the risks associated with hazardous substances and protect public health and the environment.

Q.4. Write a short note on acid rain.

Ans. Acid rain is a type of environmental pollution characterized by the deposition of acidic substances, such as sulfuric acid and nitric acid, from the atmosphere onto the Earth's surface. These acids are primarily formed through the combustion of fossil fuels and industrial activities, releasing sulfur dioxide and nitrogen oxides into the air. When these pollutants react with water vapor and atmospheric gases, they form acidic compounds that are carried by precipitation, such as rain, snow, or fog. Acid rain can damage ecosystems, soil fertility, aquatic habitats, and infrastructure, posing risks to human health and the environment.

Q.5. Environmental laboratories.

Ans. An environmental laboratory is a specialized facility equipped to analyze and assess various environmental parameters, such as air quality, water quality, soil composition, and biological contaminants. These laboratories employ advanced techniques and instruments to detect pollutants, monitor environmental trends, and ensure compliance with regulatory standards. Environmental laboratories play a crucial role in environmental monitoring, research, and risk assessment, providing valuable data and insights to government agencies, industries, and research institutions. They contribute to environmental protection efforts by identifying sources of pollution, evaluating the effectiveness of mitigation measures, and supporting evidence-based decision-making for sustainable resource management and conservation.

Q.6. What duty regarding the environment is cast on the state under article 48A of Indian Constitution?

Ans. Article 48A of the Indian Constitution casts a duty on the State to protect and improve the environment and to safeguard forests and wildlife. This constitutional provision is enshrined under the Directive Principles of State Policy, which are guiding principles for governance and policy-making.

The duty imposed by Article 48A reflects the recognition of the vital importance of environmental conservation and sustainable development in the socio-economic fabric of the nation. It underscores the State's responsibility to adopt measures aimed at preserving the environment, conserving natural resources, and promoting ecological balance for the well-being of present and future generations.

The State is expected to formulate and implement policies, laws, and programs that prioritize environmental protection and conservation efforts. This includes measures to prevent pollution, mitigate environmental degradation, conserve biodiversity, and promote sustainable development practices across various sectors of the economy.

Article 48A emphasizes the significance of safeguarding forests and wildlife, recognizing their intrinsic value and ecological significance. The State is tasked with enacting laws and policies to protect forests and wildlife habitats, prevent deforestation and habitat destruction, and promote conservation initiatives to preserve biodiversity.

Thus, Article 48A underscores the constitutional imperative for the State to proactively engage in environmental stewardship and adopt measures aimed at achieving environmental sustainability and ecological harmony.

Q.7. What are the conditions on use of certain industrial plants in air pollution control areas under sections 21(5) of the Air (Prevention and Control of Pollution) Act, 1981?

Ans. Section 21(5) of the Air (Prevention and Control of Pollution) Act, 1981, imposes certain conditions on the use of certain industrial plants located in air pollution control areas. These conditions are aimed at regulating industrial activities to mitigate air pollution and protect public health and the environment.

Compliance with Standards: Industrial plants must comply with emission standards and guidelines specified by the Central Pollution Control Board (CPCB) or State Pollution Control Board (SPCB) to limit air pollutant emissions.

Use of Pollution Control Devices: Industrial plants are required to install and operate pollution control devices, such as electrostatic precipitators, scrubbers, or particulate control systems, to reduce emissions of pollutants.

Periodic Monitoring: Industrial plants must conduct periodic monitoring of air emissions to ensure compliance with prescribed standards and regulations. Monitoring data should be reported to the relevant pollution control authorities.

Maintenance and Inspection: Industrial plants are obligated to maintain pollution control equipment in good working condition and allow regular inspections by pollution control authorities to verify compliance with regulatory requirements.

Record-Keeping: Industrial plants must maintain records of emissions, maintenance activities, and monitoring results as per the prescribed format and provide access to these records to pollution control authorities upon request.

Penalties for Non-Compliance: Non-compliance with the conditions specified under Section 21(5) may result in penalties, fines, or legal action by pollution control authorities, including closure or suspension of operations.

These conditions aim to promote pollution prevention, control, and abatement measures in industrial activities to minimize adverse impacts on air quality and public health in air pollution control areas. Compliance with these conditions is essential to ensure environmental sustainability and protect air quality for present and future generations.

Q.8. What are the rules laid down by the state government to regulate matters of protected forests? Differentiate between protected and reserve forests.

Ans. The state government lays down rules to regulate matters concerning protected forests in accordance with the provisions of relevant forest conservation laws and policies. These rules aim to ensure the conservation and sustainable management of protected forest areas. Some common rules laid down by state governments may include:

Access Restrictions: Regulations governing access to protected forest areas, including rules on entry permits, visitor quotas, and permissible activities.

Resource Use: Guidelines for sustainable resource utilization within protected forests, such as rules on timber harvesting, non-timber forest product collection, and grazing rights.

Wildlife Conservation: Measures for wildlife protection and habitat conservation, including rules on hunting, poaching, and habitat disturbance.

Fire Management: Protocols for preventing and managing forest fires, including restrictions on firewood collection and guidelines for controlled burning practices.

Community Participation: Policies promoting community involvement in protected forest management through participatory decision-making, collaborative conservation initiatives, and community-based ecotourism.

Q.9. Differentiating between protected and reserve forests:

Protected Forests: Protected forests are designated areas managed for the conservation of biodiversity, ecosystem services, and cultural heritage. They may allow for some sustainable resource use and regulated human activities, such as ecotourism and scientific research.

Reserve Forests: Reserve forests, on the other hand, are areas strictly protected from human interference and resource extraction. They are managed primarily for conservation purposes and may have stricter regulations on access and resource utilization. Reserve forests serve as important biodiversity hotspots and provide critical habitats for wildlife species.

Q.10. Explain the rules of regulate environmental pollution under environmental (Protection) Act, 1986.

Ans. The Environmental Protection Act, 1986, provides a comprehensive framework for regulating and controlling environmental pollution in India. The Act empowers the central government to formulate policies and regulations to prevent and mitigate pollution and protect the environment. Some key rules laid down under the Environmental Protection Act, 1986, to regulate environmental pollution include:

Setting Standards: The Act empowers the central government to establish standards for emission and discharge of pollutants into the environment, including air, water, and soil.

Regulatory Authorities: The Act establishes regulatory authorities, such as the Central Pollution Control Board (CPCB) at the national level and State Pollution Control Boards (SPCBs) at the state level, to enforce environmental laws and regulations, monitor pollution levels, and implement pollution control measures.

Pollution Control Measures: The Act outlines measures for pollution control and prevention, including the installation of pollution control devices, treatment of industrial effluents and emissions, and adoption of best practices for pollution prevention.

Pollution Monitoring: The Act mandates regular monitoring and assessment of pollution levels in air, water, and soil through monitoring networks and surveillance programs conducted by regulatory authorities.

Compliance and Enforcement: The Act provides for penalties, fines, and legal action against polluting industries and individuals found in violation of environmental laws and regulations. It also empowers regulatory authorities to issue closure orders, impose fines, and prosecute offenders to ensure compliance with pollution control measures.

Thus, the Environmental Protection Act, 1986, serves as a crucial legal framework for regulating environmental pollution, promoting sustainable development, and protecting the environment and public health in India.

Q.11. Noise is a nuisance in penal code and a health hazard in environmental laws. Comment.

Ans. Noise pollution is a multifaceted issue that impacts both public health and quality of life, warranting attention from both legal and environmental perspectives. In the penal code, noise is classified as a nuisance under Section 268, which addresses acts that cause annoyance or injury to the public. Excessive noise disturbances, such as loud music, construction activities, or industrial operations, can disrupt peace and tranquility, infringe upon individuals' rights to quiet enjoyment, and constitute a legal nuisance under criminal law.

Additionally, noise is recognized as a significant health hazard under environmental laws and regulations. Prolonged exposure to high levels of noise pollution can lead to various adverse health effects, including hearing loss, cardiovascular problems, stress, sleep disturbances, and decreased cognitive function. As such, environmental laws, such as the Environment (Protection) Act, 1986, and Noise Pollution (Regulation and Control) Rules, 2000, aim to mitigate noise pollution and protect public health by establishing standards for permissible noise levels, regulating noise-emitting activities, and prescribing measures for noise control and abatement.

The dual characterization of noise as both a legal nuisance and a health hazard underscores the need for comprehensive measures to address this issue. Effective enforcement of noise regulations, public awareness campaigns, community engagement, and technological innovations in noise control are essential to mitigate noise pollution's adverse impacts and promote a healthier and more harmonious living environment.

Q.12. Explain in detail the concept of sustainable development. What role has Indian Supreme Court played in making it applicable in India? Discuss.

Ans. Sustainable development is a holistic approach to economic, social, and environmental progress that seeks to meet the needs of the present without compromising the ability of future generations to meet their own needs. It emphasizes the integration of economic growth, social equity, and environmental protection to ensure long-term prosperity and well-being for all. Sustainable development aims to balance the three pillars of sustainability: economic development, social equity, and environmental protection, to achieve harmony between human activities and the natural environment.

The Indian Supreme Court has played a significant role in advancing the concept of sustainable development and making it applicable in India through its judicial activism and landmark judgments. The Court has interpreted the right to a healthy environment as a fundamental right under Article 21 of the Indian Constitution, encompassing the principles of sustainable development. In several cases, such as Vellore Citizens Welfare Forum v. Union of India and M.C. Mehta v. Union of India, the Supreme Court has emphasized the importance of sustainable development and environmental protection, issuing directives to industries, governments, and regulatory bodies to adopt measures to mitigate pollution, conserve natural resources, and promote sustainable development practices.

Thus, the Court has employed the principle of public trust doctrine to safeguard environmental resources and ensure their sustainable use for the benefit of present and future generations. By incorporating principles of sustainable development into its jurisprudence, the Indian Supreme Court has played a pivotal role in promoting environmental sustainability, enhancing environmental governance, and advancing the cause of sustainable development in India.

Write a detailed note on Public Interest Litigation and environmental protection in India. Mention the contribution of M.C. Mehta in protection of environment.

Ans. Public Interest Litigation (PIL) has emerged as a powerful tool for promoting environmental protection and advancing the cause of sustainable development in India. PIL allows any citizen or organization to approach the courts on behalf of the public interest, seeking judicial intervention to address issues of environmental degradation, pollution, and ecological harm. It enables the judiciary to adjudicate matters of environmental concern and enforce environmental laws and regulations effectively.

One of the most prominent figures in the realm of environmental protection through PIL in India is M.C. Mehta, an environmental activist and lawyer. Mehta has filed numerous PILs over the years, highlighting environmental issues and advocating for their resolution through judicial intervention. His efforts have led to several landmark judgments that have significantly contributed to environmental conservation and sustainable development in India.

One of Mehta's notable contributions is the case of M.C. Mehta v. Union of India (1986), commonly known as the Oleum Gas Leak case. In this case, Mehta filed a PIL seeking the closure of a hazardous chemical plant in Delhi that posed a serious risk to public health and the environment. The Supreme Court, recognizing the urgency of the matter, issued directives to the plant to implement safety measures and ultimately ordered its closure. This judgment set a precedent for judicial activism in environmental matters and underscored the judiciary's role in safeguarding public health and the environment.

Mehta's efforts have also led to significant interventions in cases related to vehicular pollution, industrial pollution, river pollution, and forest conservation, among others. His tireless advocacy through PILs has contributed to the strengthening of environmental laws, enforcement mechanisms, and institutional frameworks for environmental governance in India. Mehta's work exemplifies the instrumental role of PIL in promoting environmental justice, holding authorities accountable, and advancing the cause of environmental protection in the country.

Environmental Law 2018 Question Paper

Q.1. Define the Environment.

Ans. The environment encompasses the sum total of all living and nonliving components of the Earth, including the atmosphere, hydrosphere, lithosphere, and biosphere. It encompasses the air we breathe, the water we drink, the land we inhabit, and the biodiversity that thrives within it. The environment provides the essential resources and conditions necessary for life to exist, including food, water, shelter, and climate stability. It is characterized by complex interactions and interdependencies between various natural systems and human activities, shaping ecosystems, habitats, and landscapes. Protecting and preserving the environment is vital for sustaining life, fostering biodiversity, and ensuring the well-being of present and future generations.

Q.2. What is the purpose of the Constitution of an area as a National Park?

Ans. The purpose of designating an area as a National Park is to preserve and protect its natural beauty, biodiversity, and ecological integrity. National Parks are established to conserve unique and representative ecosystems, habitats, and species, ensuring their long-term survival and providing opportunities for scientific research, education, and recreation. By restricting human activities and development within their boundaries, National Parks aim to maintain the natural processes and ecological balance of the area while allowing visitors to experience and appreciate its scenic and biological treasures. Overall, the designation of an area as a National Park serves to safeguard natural heritage and promote environmental conservation for future generations.

Q.3. What is the main function of Central Zoo authority?

Ans. The main function of the Central Zoo Authority (CZA) is to regulate and oversee the establishment and management of zoos in India. It sets standards and guidelines for the maintenance, housing, and care of animals in captivity, ensuring their welfare and well-being. The CZA grants recognition to zoos that comply with its guidelines and provides financial assistance for their development and improvement. Additionally, it conducts inspections and evaluations of zoos to ensure compliance with regulatory standards and takes corrective measures to address deficiencies or violations. Overall, the CZA plays a crucial role in promoting the ethical and sustainable management of zoos across India.

Q.4. What is radioactive pollution?

Ans. Radioactive pollution refers to the contamination of the environment by radioactive materials, such as radioactive isotopes of elements like uranium, thorium, and radium. This pollution occurs when radioactive substances are released into the air, water, or soil through human activities such as nuclear accidents, nuclear weapons testing, nuclear power plant operations, or improper disposal of radioactive waste. Radioactive pollution poses significant health and environmental risks as exposure to ionizing radiation can cause genetic mutations, cancer, birth defects, and other serious health problems. Effective management and containment of radioactive materials are essential to prevent further contamination and mitigate the adverse impacts of radioactive pollution.

Q.5. What are the Hazardous Substances? Discuss.

Ans. Hazardous substances are materials that pose a threat to human health, the environment, or property due to their chemical, physical, or biological properties. These substances include toxic chemicals, flammable liquids, corrosive agents, radioactive materials, and biological pathogens. Exposure to hazardous substances can result in acute or chronic health effects, including poisoning, respiratory ailments, cancer, or reproductive disorders. Additionally, hazardous substances can cause environmental pollution, soil and water contamination, and ecological harm. Effective management and regulation of hazardous substances is essential to minimize risks to human health and the environment and ensure safe handling, storage, and disposal practices.

Q.6. Discuss the provision relating to protect the environment under Indian Constitution.

Ans. Under the Indian Constitution, environmental protection is enshrined primarily under Article 48A and Article 51A(g). Article 48A directs the State to endeavor to protect and improve the environment and safeguard forests and wildlife. Article 51A(g) imposes a fundamental duty on citizens to protect and improve the natural environment including forests, lakes, rivers, and wildlife, and to have compassion for living creatures. These constitutional provisions underscore the importance of environmental conservation and sustainable development, guiding legislative and policy measures to mitigate environmental degradation and promote ecological sustainability in India.

Q.7. Define Hazardous Substances. What are the precautions taken before handling Hazardous substances?

Ans. Hazardous substances are materials that possess properties capable of causing harm to human health, the environment, or property. These substances include toxic chemicals, flammable liquids, corrosive agents, radioactive materials, and biological pathogens. Exposure to hazardous substances can lead to acute or chronic health effects, such as poisoning, respiratory ailments, cancer, or reproductive disorders. Additionally, hazardous substances can cause environmental pollution, soil and water contamination, and ecological harm.

Precautions taken before handling hazardous substances include:

Identification: Proper identification and labeling of hazardous substances to ensure awareness of potential risks.

Training: Adequate training for personnel involved in handling hazardous substances to understand safe handling procedures and emergency response protocols.

Personal Protective Equipment (PPE): Use of appropriate PPE, such as gloves, goggles, masks, and protective clothing, to minimize exposure to hazardous substances.

Ventilation: Ensuring adequate ventilation in areas where hazardous substances are handled to prevent the buildup of fumes, vapors, or dust.

Containment: Use of spill containment measures, such as secondary containment systems and absorbent materials, to prevent accidental release of hazardous substances.

Storage: Proper storage of hazardous substances in designated areas with appropriate containment measures and segregation from incompatible materials.

Emergency Response: Establishment of emergency response procedures, including evacuation routes, spill response protocols, and communication channels, to address accidents or incidents involving hazardous substances promptly and effectively.

Q.8. What are the functions and powers of the Central and State Pollution Control Board? Comment.

Ans. The Central Pollution Control Board (CPCB) and State Pollution Control Boards (SPCBs) are statutory bodies established under the Water (Prevention and Control of Pollution) Act, 1974, and the Air (Prevention and Control of Pollution) Act, 1981.

Functions and Powers of CPCB:

Setting and enforcing national standards for air and water quality.

Coordinating and supervising the activities of SPCBs.

Conducting research and studies on pollution control.

Providing technical assistance and guidance to SPCBs.

Monitoring and assessing environmental quality at the national level.

Investigating and enforcing regulations related to environmental pollution.

Functions and Powers of SPCBs:

Implementing pollution control laws and regulations at the state level.

Granting consent to operate and consent to establish for industries.

Conducting inspections and monitoring air and water quality.

Enforcing pollution control standards and guidelines.

Investigating complaints and incidents of environmental pollution.

Comment: While CPCB sets national standards and guidelines, SPCBs play a crucial role in implementing and enforcing pollution control measures at the state level. However, challenges such as inadequate resources and enforcement gaps need to be addressed for more effective pollution control and environmental management. Collaboration between CPCB, SPCBs, industries, and civil society is essential for achieving sustainable development and ensuring a cleaner environment.

Q.9. What is the contribution of Public Interest Litigation to protect the environment?

Ans. Public Interest Litigation (PIL) has been instrumental in protecting the environment by providing a platform for citizens and environmental activists to raise concerns and seek judicial intervention to address environmental issues. PIL allows individuals and organizations to petition the courts on behalf of the public interest, leading to landmark judgments and directives that have significantly contributed to environmental conservation and sustainable development.

PIL has facilitated the enforcement of environmental laws and regulations, ensuring compliance with statutory provisions and holding authorities accountable for environmental degradation. Through PIL, courts have addressed a wide range of environmental issues, including air and water pollution, deforestation, wildlife conservation, and waste management. PIL has played a crucial role in raising awareness about environmental issues and mobilizing public support for environmental protection initiatives. It has empowered communities to advocate for their environmental rights and participate in decision-making processes related to environmental governance.

PIL has catalyzed policy reform and legislative action by highlighting gaps and deficiencies in existing environmental laws and regulations. It has spurred government agencies to take proactive measures to address environmental concerns and implement sustainable development initiatives.

Thus, PIL has been a powerful tool for advancing the cause of environmental protection, promoting environmental justice, and ensuring the well-being of present and future generations.

Q.10. What are the disqualification of a person to be a member of a Board Constituted under Water (Prevention and Control of Pollution) Act 1974?

Ans. Under the Water (Prevention and Control of Pollution) Act, 1974, certain disqualifications are specified for individuals who wish to become members of a Board constituted under the Act. These disqualifications aim to ensure the integrity, impartiality, and effectiveness of the Board in fulfilling its functions related to water pollution control and prevention.

The disqualifications for a person to be a member of such a Board include:

Holding Office of Profit: A person who holds any office of profit under the central or state government is disqualified from being a member of the Board. This provision prevents conflicts of interest and ensures the independence of the Board from governmental influence.

Conviction for Offenses: Individuals who have been convicted of an offense involving moral turpitude are disqualified from serving as members of the Board. This requirement aims to maintain the integrity and reputation of the Board by barring individuals with a history of criminal conduct.

Unsuitability: Any person who is declared to be unsuitable by the central or state government due to reasons such as misconduct, incompetence, or conflict of interest may be disqualified from serving as a member of the Board. This provision allows authorities to prevent individuals who may compromise the objectives and functions of the Board from holding membership.

These disqualifications help ensure that members of the Board possess the necessary integrity, competence, and commitment to fulfill their responsibilities effectively in safeguarding water resources and preventing water pollution.

Q.11. Explain in detail the concept of Sustainable development.

Ans. Sustainable development is a holistic approach to economic, social, and environmental progress that seeks to meet the needs of the present without compromising the ability of future generations to meet their own needs. It involves balancing economic growth with social equity and environmental conservation to ensure long-term prosperity and well-being for all. Sustainable development aims to integrate economic development, social inclusion, and environmental protection to achieve harmony between human activities and the natural environment. It emphasizes the importance of resource efficiency, environmental stewardship, and social justice in promoting a resilient and equitable society. Sustainable development recognizes the interconnectedness of social, economic, and environmental systems and seeks to address global challenges such as poverty, inequality, and climate change through integrated and collaborative approaches.

Q.12. Ozone layer depletion is causing Damage to the environment. Comment.

Ans. Ozone layer depletion is a critical environmental issue with far-reaching consequences. The ozone layer acts as Earth's shield, protecting life from harmful ultraviolet (UV) radiation from the sun. However, human activities, particularly the release of ozone-depleting substances (ODS) such as chlorofluorocarbons (CFCs) and halons, have led to the thinning of the ozone layer. This depletion allows more UV radiation to reach the Earth's surface, resulting in adverse effects on human health, ecosystems, and the environment.

Increased UV radiation can cause skin cancer, cataracts, and immune system suppression in humans. It can also harm marine organisms, plants, and ecosystems, leading to reduced crop yields, disruption of food chains, and loss of biodiversity. Moreover, ozone depletion contributes to climate change by altering atmospheric circulation patterns and exacerbating global warming. Addressing ozone layer depletion requires international cooperation, strict regulation of ODS, and concerted efforts to promote sustainable practices and technologies.

What are the major International Treaties on Environmental Protection? What measures has India adopted to comply with them? Discuss.

Ans. Several major international treaties and agreements have been established to address various environmental issues and promote global cooperation in environmental protection. Some of the key treaties include:

United Nations Framework Convention on Climate Change (UNFCCC): Aimed at addressing climate change and reducing greenhouse gas emissions.

Kyoto Protocol: An extension of the UNFCCC, setting binding emission reduction targets for developed countries.

Paris Agreement: A landmark agreement under the UNFCCC, committing countries to limit global warming to well below 2 degrees Celsius above pre-industrial levels.

Montreal Protocol: Designed to protect the ozone layer by phasing out the production and use of ozone-depleting substances (ODS).

Convention on Biological Diversity (CBD): Seeks to conserve biodiversity, promote sustainable use of biological resources, and ensure fair and equitable sharing of benefits.

Stockholm Convention on Persistent Organic Pollutants (POPs): Aims to eliminate or restrict the production and use of persistent organic pollutants, which pose significant risks to human health and the environment.

India has taken several measures to comply with these international treaties and agreements:

Ratification and Implementation: India has ratified most of these treaties and agreements, demonstrating its commitment to global environmental protection efforts.

National Action Plans: India has developed national action plans and strategies to address specific environmental issues outlined in these treaties, such as climate change, biodiversity conservation, and ozone layer protection.

Policy Formulation: India has formulated environmental policies and regulations aligned with the objectives of these treaties, such as the National Action Plan on Climate Change, National Biodiversity Action Plan, and Ozone Depleting Substances (Regulation and Control) Rules.

Capacity Building and Technology Transfer: India has engaged in capacity building initiatives and technology transfer programs to enhance its ability to implement and comply with international environmental obligations.

Multilateral Cooperation: India actively participates in multilateral forums and negotiations to contribute to the development and implementation of global environmental agreements while advocating for the interests of developing countries.

Overall, India's efforts to comply with international environmental treaties demonstrate its commitment to global environmental stewardship and sustainable development.

Q.13. Discuss the Power of State Government to Supersede the State Board Under Air (Prevention and control of pollution) Act 1981.

Ans. Under the Air (Prevention and Control of Pollution) Act, 1981, the State Government possesses the power to supersede the State Pollution Control Board (SPCB) under certain circumstances. Section 31 of the Act outlines the conditions and procedures for the exercise of this power.

Grounds for Supersession: The State Government may supersede the SPCB if it is satisfied that the Board has persistently defaulted in the performance of its duties or has exceeded or abused its powers. This provision allows the State Government to intervene when the functioning of the SPCB is deemed inadequate or problematic.

Notification: The State Government must issue a notification specifying the reasons for the proposed supersession and appoint an officer or authority to perform the functions of the SPCB during the period of supersession.

Duration: The supersession may initially last for a period of not exceeding six months. However, the State Government may extend this period for an additional period or periods, each not exceeding six months in total.

Dissolution of the Board: If the SPCB is not reconstituted before the expiry of the supersession period or the extended period, all the members of the Board shall vacate their offices, and the Board shall be deemed to have been dissolved.

Reconstitution: Following the supersession, the State Government must reconstitute the SPCB within the stipulated time frame, ensuring the appointment of competent and qualified individuals to carry out the functions of the Board effectively.

The power of the State Government to supersede the SPCB serves as a mechanism to address instances of persistent non-performance, abuse of power, or dysfunctionality within the Board, thereby ensuring the efficient and effective regulation of air pollution control measures at the state level. However, this power must be exercised judiciously and in accordance with the provisions of the Act to uphold principles of good governance and environmental protection.

Environmental Law 2017 Question Paper

Q.1. Define the Environment.

Ans. The environment refers to the surroundings and conditions in which living organisms, including humans, exist. It encompasses both natural and human-made elements, including the air, water, land, flora, fauna, and ecosystems. The environment provides essential resources and services necessary for life, such as clean air, water, food, and habitat. It also includes the interactions and interdependencies between living organisms and their surroundings. Protection and preservation of the environment are crucial for sustaining life, promoting biodiversity, mitigating climate change, and ensuring the well-being of present and future generations.

Q.2. What is radioactive pollution?

Ans. A radioactive pollutant is a substance that emits ionizing radiation due to its unstable atomic nucleus. These pollutants can contaminate the environment through various sources, such as nuclear power plants, industrial processes, medical facilities, and nuclear weapons testing. Examples of radioactive pollutants include isotopes of elements like uranium, thorium, radium, and cesium. Exposure to radioactive pollutants poses significant health risks, including increased cancer rates, genetic mutations, and other adverse health effects. Effective management and containment of radioactive pollutants are essential to prevent environmental contamination and minimize the risks to human health and ecosystems.

Q.3. What is the main function of Zoo Authority?

Ans. The main function of the zoo authority is to regulate and oversee the establishment, management, and functioning of zoos across the country. It sets standards and guidelines for the housing, care, and welfare of animals in captivity, ensuring their well-being and safety. The authority grants recognition to zoos that comply with its regulations and provides technical assistance and guidance for their development and improvement. Additionally, the zoo authority conducts inspections and assessments to monitor compliance with standards and takes corrective measures to address deficiencies or violations, thereby promoting ethical and sustainable practices in zoo management.

Q.4. What is Carbon Trading?

Ans. Carbon trading, also known as emissions trading, is a market-based mechanism designed to reduce greenhouse gas emissions. Under this system, governments or regulatory bodies set a cap on the total amount of emissions that industries or organizations are allowed to produce. Companies that emit less than their allocated limit can sell their unused allowances as carbon credits to those that exceed their limit. This creates a financial incentive for industries to reduce their emissions and invest in cleaner technologies. Carbon trading aims to mitigate climate change by incentivizing emissions reductions while promoting economic efficiency and innovation in low-carbon technologies.

Q.5. What do you understand by Acid rain?

Ans. Acid rain is a type of precipitation that occurs when atmospheric pollutants, such as sulfur dioxide (SO2) and nitrogen oxides (NOx), react with water vapor in the atmosphere to form sulfuric acid (H2SO4) and nitric acid (HNO3). These acidic compounds then fall to the ground in the form of rain, snow, fog, or dust particles. Acid rain can have detrimental effects on the environment, including the acidification of soil and water bodies, damage to vegetation, aquatic ecosystems, and infrastructure, and adverse impacts on human health. It is often caused by emissions from industrial processes, vehicle exhaust, and fossil fuel combustion.

Q.6. Ozone Layer depletion is causing damage to the environment. Comment.

Ans. Ozone layer depletion is a critical environmental issue with severe consequences. The ozone layer shields the Earth from harmful ultraviolet (UV) radiation, but human activities, particularly the release of ozone-depleting substances (ODS) like chlorofluorocarbons (CFCs) and halons, have led to its thinning. This depletion allows more UV radiation to reach the Earth's surface, resulting in adverse effects on human health, ecosystems, and the environment. Increased UV radiation can cause skin cancer, cataracts, and harm to marine organisms and crops. Addressing ozone layer depletion requires global cooperation, strict regulation of ODS, and promotion of sustainable practices to mitigate its harmful impacts.

Q.7. Discuss the provisions relating to protecting the environment under Indian Constitution.

Ans. The Indian Constitution incorporates provisions aimed at protecting the environment to ensure sustainable development. Article 48A directs the State to safeguard forests, wildlife, and the environment. Article 51A(g) imposes a fundamental duty on citizens to protect and improve the natural environment, including forests, rivers, and wildlife. These constitutional provisions underscore the significance of environmental conservation and sustainable development, guiding legislative and policy measures to mitigate environmental degradation and promote ecological sustainability in India. Additionally, various environmental laws and regulations have been enacted to implement these constitutional mandates and address specific environmental concerns across the country.

Q.8. Discuss the objects of the constitution of an area as a National Park.

Ans. The establishment of an area as a National Park serves several key objectives aimed at conservation, preservation, and sustainable management of natural resources. Firstly, National Parks are designated to protect and conserve unique ecosystems, habitats, and species of flora and fauna, thereby safeguarding biodiversity and maintaining ecological balance. Secondly, they provide opportunities for scientific research, education, and interpretation, facilitating the study of natural processes and promoting environmental awareness and appreciation among visitors. Thirdly, National Parks offer recreational opportunities for visitors to experience and enjoy nature, promoting outdoor recreation and tourism while ensuring the preservation of natural landscapes and cultural heritage. Additionally, National Parks contribute to watershed protection, soil conservation, and climate regulation, enhancing the overall quality of the environment and promoting sustainable development. Overall, the objects of constituting an area as a National Park aim to fulfill conservation, education, recreation, and environmental stewardship objectives for the benefit of present and future generations.

Q.9. Define Hazardous substances. What are the precautions taken before handling hazardous substances?

Ans. Hazardous substances are materials that possess properties capable of causing harm to human health, the environment, or property. These substances include toxic chemicals, flammable liquids, corrosive agents, radioactive materials, and biological pathogens. Exposure to hazardous substances can lead to acute or chronic health effects, such as poisoning, respiratory ailments, cancer, or reproductive disorders. Additionally, hazardous substances can cause environmental pollution, soil and water contamination, and ecological harm.

Precautions taken before handling hazardous substances are crucial to minimize risks and ensure safety. These precautions include:

Identification: Properly identifying hazardous substances and understanding their potential risks.

Training: Providing adequate training for personnel on safe handling procedures, emergency response protocols, and the use of personal protective equipment (PPE).

Personal Protective Equipment (PPE): Using appropriate PPE such as gloves, goggles, masks, and protective clothing to minimize exposure.

Ventilation: Ensuring proper ventilation in areas where hazardous substances are handled to prevent the buildup of fumes, vapors, or dust.

Containment: Implementing spill containment measures to prevent accidental release and minimize environmental contamination.

Storage: Storing hazardous substances in designated areas with appropriate containment measures and segregation from incompatible materials.

Emergency Response: Establishing procedures for responding to accidents or incidents involving hazardous substances, including evacuation routes, spill response protocols, and communication channels.

Q.10. What are the provisions relating to prohibition on use of streams or well for disposal of matter etc.? under the water (Prevention and control of Pollution) Act, 1974?

Ans. Under the Water (Prevention and Control of Pollution) Act, 1974, provisions are outlined to prohibit the use of streams or wells for the disposal of matter or for sewage effluent. Section 24 of the Act stipulates the following provisions:

Prohibition on Disposal: No person shall knowingly cause or permit any poisonous, noxious, or polluting matter to enter into any stream or well. This provision aims to prevent the contamination of water bodies by prohibiting the discharge of harmful substances into streams or wells.

Exceptions: The Act allows for certain exceptions to the prohibition, provided that prior consent has been obtained from the State Pollution Control Board or Pollution Control Committee. These exceptions may be granted for activities such as research or experiments conducted in the public interest or for any other purpose considered necessary by the Board or Committee.

Offenses and Penalties: Any person who contravenes the provisions of Section 24 shall be punishable with imprisonment for a term extending up to three months, or with a fine that may extend to ten thousand rupees, or with both.

These provisions aim to prevent water pollution and protect water resources by regulating the disposal of harmful substances into streams or wells, thereby ensuring the availability of clean and safe water for various purposes, including drinking, irrigation, and industrial use.

Q.11. Discuss the provision regarding the constitution of the State Board for prevention and control of Air Pollution. Explain the terms and conditions of Service of members. What is the disqualification of members?

Ans. The provision regarding the constitution of the State Board for the Prevention and Control of Air Pollution is outlined in the Air (Prevention and Control of Pollution) Act, 1981. According to Section 3 of the Act, the State Government shall constitute a State Pollution Control Board, which shall be responsible for implementing the provisions of the Act within the state.

Terms and Conditions of Service of Members:

Composition: The State Pollution Control Board consists of a full-time chairman, a member-secretary, and such number of other members as may be deemed necessary by the State Government.

Appointment: Members of the State Board, including the chairman and member-secretary, are appointed by the State Government.

Tenure: Members of the State Board serve for a term of three years, which may be extended by the State Government.

Qualifications: Members of the State Board are appointed based on their qualifications, expertise, and experience in fields relevant to pollution control, environmental science, public health, or engineering.

Removal: Members may be removed from office by the State Government if they are found to be incapable, ineffective, or guilty of misconduct.

Disqualifications of Members:

Holding Office of Profit: Members of the State Board cannot hold any office of profit under the State Government or the Central Government.

Conflict of Interest: Individuals who have a financial or other interest that may conflict with the duties of a member of the State Board may be disqualified from serving as members.

Conviction for Offenses: Persons convicted of offenses involving moral turpitude are disqualified from being members of the State Board.

These provisions ensure that members of the State Pollution Control Board possess the necessary qualifications, integrity, and commitment to effectively carry out their responsibilities in preventing and controlling air pollution within the state.

Q.12. How is protection of Specified plants made under Wild Life (Protection) Act, 1972?

Ans. The protection of specified plants under the Wild Life (Protection) Act, 1972 is primarily achieved through the declaration of certain areas as protected areas, such as national parks, wildlife sanctuaries, and biosphere reserves. Additionally, the Act provides specific provisions for the protection of endangered and threatened plant species, including the following measures:

Prohibition of Collection and Trade: The Act prohibits the hunting, killing, or capture of specified plants listed in Schedules I to VI of the Act without prior permission from the Chief Wildlife Warden or authorized officer. It also prohibits the possession, sale, or transport of any part or derivative of such plants.

Declaration of Protected Plants: The Act empowers the Central Government to declare any plant species as a "protected plant" through notification in the Official Gazette. Once designated as protected, stringent regulations are imposed on the collection, trade, and use of these plants to prevent their exploitation and depletion.

Regulation of Trade and Export: The Act regulates the trade and export of specified plants through the issuance of licenses and permits. It mandates the establishment of authorities at the state and central levels to monitor and control the trade in protected plants, ensuring compliance with the provisions of the Act.

Establishment of Botanical Gardens: The Act encourages the establishment of botanical gardens for the conservation and propagation of endangered plant species. These gardens serve as repositories of genetic diversity and play a crucial role in ex-situ conservation efforts.

The Wild Life (Protection) Act, 1972 provides a comprehensive legal framework for the conservation and protection of specified plants, contributing to the preservation of biodiversity and the sustainable management of natural resources.

Q.13. What are protected forests? State the power of the State Government to make rules for protected forests.

Ans. Protected forests are areas of forest land that are legally designated and managed for the purpose of conservation and sustainable use of forest resources. These forests are afforded special protection under the forest laws of a country to ensure their ecological integrity, biodiversity conservation, and sustainable management. In India, protected forests are categorized into different classes, including reserved forests, protected forests, and village forests, each with specific management objectives and legal provisions.

The power of the State Government to make rules for protected forests is conferred under the Indian Forest Act, 1927. Section 30 of the Act empowers the State Government to make rules for the following purposes:

Regulation of Entry and Movement: The State Government can make rules to regulate and control entry into protected forests, movement within such forests, and the collection of forest produce by individuals or communities.

Protection of Forests: Rules may be formulated to prevent and suppress forest offenses such as unauthorized felling of trees, illegal grazing, encroachment, poaching, and forest fires within protected forests.

Management and Utilization: The State Government can prescribe rules governing the management, use, and exploitation of forest resources within protected forests, including the issuance of permits for timber extraction, grazing rights, and other forest-related activities.

Preservation of Wildlife: Rules may be enacted to protect and conserve wildlife species found within protected forests, including the establishment of wildlife sanctuaries and reserves, regulation of hunting and trapping, and protection of habitats.

Administrative Matters: Rules may also cover administrative matters such as the appointment and functions of forest officers, establishment of forest offices, and revenue collection.

These rules are essential for the effective management and conservation of protected forests, ensuring their sustainable utilization while safeguarding ecological values and biodiversity. They provide the legal framework for regulating human activities within protected forest areas and promoting the long-term sustainability of forest ecosystems.

CHAPTER FOUR

Banking and Negotiable Instruments Act

Banking Law 2023 Question Paper

Q.1. Define Holder in Due Course.

Ans. A Holder in Due Course refers to a person who acquires a negotiable instrument, such as a promissory note or bill of exchange, in good faith, for value, and without notice of any defects or irregularities. To qualify as an Holder in Due Course, the individual must meet specific criteria outlined in the law, including acquiring the instrument for consideration, taking it in good faith without knowledge of any defects, and obtaining it before it is overdue. An Holder in Due Course enjoys certain legal protections and rights, including immunity from certain defenses that could be raised against a regular holder.

Q.2. What do you understand by cheque?

Ans. A cheque is a negotiable instrument used in banking transactions to facilitate the transfer of funds from one party to another. It is a written order, typically issued by an account holder (the drawer) to their bank, instructing the bank to pay a specified sum of money to the person or entity named on the cheque (the payee). Cheques are commonly used for various purposes, including making payments, settling debts, and conducting business transactions. They provide a convenient and secure method of transferring funds, allowing for easy verification and record-keeping by both the payer and the payee.

Q.3. Define Banker.

Ans. A banker is a financial institution or individual engaged in the business of providing banking services, such as accepting deposits, lending money, and facilitating financial transactions. Banks typically offer a range of services to their customers, including current and savings accounts, loans, mortgages, and investment products. They act as custodians of money, providing a safe and secure environment for individuals and businesses to deposit and withdraw funds, as well as access various financial services. Banks also play a crucial role in the economy by facilitating the flow of funds between savers and borrowers, thereby contributing to economic growth and development.

Q.4. Define Customer.

Ans. A customer is an individual, organization, or entity that engages with a business or service provider to purchase goods or services, obtain assistance, or seek solutions to their needs. In the context of banking, a customer is someone who maintains an account or conducts financial transactions with a bank. Customers may open various types of accounts, such as savings accounts, current accounts, or investment accounts, and utilize banking services offered by the institution. They interact with the bank to deposit and withdraw funds, apply for loans, request financial advice, and access other banking products and services tailored to their requirements.

Q.5. Define Negotiable Instrument.

Ans. A negotiable instrument is a document that promises or orders the payment of a specific amount of money to a designated person or bearer. It serves as a means of transferring financial rights and obligations between parties. The key characteristic of negotiable instruments is their transferability, allowing for easy and secure transactions. Common types of negotiable instruments include promissory notes, bills of exchange, and cheques. These instruments are governed by specific legal frameworks, such as the Negotiable Instruments Act, which outline their requirements, features, and regulations to ensure their validity and enforceability in commercial transactions.

Q.6. Describe the privileges of a 'Holder in due course'?

Ans. A Holder in Due Course enjoys certain privileges and protections under the law, which enhance their rights as compared to a regular holder of a negotiable instrument. Some of the privileges of an Holder in Due Course include:

Holder's Status: An Holder in Due Course holds a superior position compared to other holders, entitling them to enforce the instrument and claim payment without being subject to certain defenses that could be raised against a regular holder.

Good Title: An Holder in Due Course acquires a good title to the instrument, meaning they possess lawful ownership rights that are not affected by any defects or claims against the instrument prior to its acquisition.

Protection from Defenses: An Holder in Due Course is immune from certain defenses, such as forgery, fraud, or lack of consideration, allowing them to enforce the instrument against parties who may have defenses against a regular holder.

These privileges ensure the integrity of negotiable instruments and promote confidence in commercial transactions by providing enhanced protection to bona fide holders who acquire instruments in good faith and for value.

Q.7. Elucidate the concept of Banker's Lien?

Ans. Banker's lien is a legal right that allows a bank to retain possession of a customer's funds or assets held in the bank's custody until the customer fulfills their financial obligations to the bank. It serves as a form of security for the bank against unpaid debts or liabilities owed by the customer. The lien arises automatically by operation of law, without the need for any formal agreement, when the customer's account becomes overdrawn or in default. The bank can exercise its lien by withholding funds or refusing to release assets until the outstanding debt is settled. Banker's lien applies to all types of accounts held by the customer, including savings, current, and deposit accounts, and is recognized under common law principles.

Q.8. Explain the salient features of the Banking Companies Act, 1934.

Ans. The Banking Companies Act, 1949, is an important legislation governing the operations and functioning of banking companies in India. Some of its salient features are:

Licensing and Regulation: The Act provides for the licensing and regulation of banking companies by the Reserve Bank of India (RBI), which grants licenses to entities seeking to conduct banking business in India.

Capital Requirements: It mandates banking companies to maintain minimum capital adequacy ratios to ensure their financial stability and soundness.

Branch Expansion: The Act regulates the opening of new branches by banking companies, ensuring that expansion is done in a controlled manner and in compliance with RBI guidelines.

Corporate Governance: It establishes rules and guidelines for corporate governance within banking companies, including the composition of the board of directors, their qualifications, and responsibilities.

Regulatory Oversight: The Act grants extensive powers to the RBI to supervise and regulate banking companies, including conducting inspections, issuing directives, and imposing penalties for non-compliance.

Amendment and Enforcement: The Act allows for amendments to be made to its provisions as necessary and provides mechanisms for enforcement through legal proceedings and penalties for violations.

Overall, the Banking Companies Act, 1949, plays a crucial role in ensuring the stability, integrity, and efficiency of the banking sector in India.

Q.9. What do you understand about the Dishonour of Cheque? Explain it with the help of decided cases.

Ans. The dishonor of a cheque occurs when the bank refuses to honor or pay the amount specified on the cheque presented for payment. This refusal may be due to various reasons, such as insufficient funds, irregular signature, or a stop-payment instruction issued by the drawer of the cheque.

One significant case illustrating the legal implications of dishonored cheques is "M/s NEPC Micon Ltd. & Anr. v. M/s Global Coal and Mining Pvt. Ltd. & Anr." In this case, the Supreme Court of India emphasized the seriousness of dishonored cheques and affirmed that such dishonor constitutes an offense under Section 138 of the Negotiable

Instruments Act, 1881. The court held that the drawer of a dishonored cheque is liable to criminal prosecution and can be punished with imprisonment and/or a fine.

Another notable case is "Dashrath Rupsingh Rathod v. State of Maharashtra," where the Supreme Court clarified that the liability under Section 138 of the Negotiable Instruments Act arises only when the dishonored cheque is presented within the validity period or within six months from the date it was drawn, whichever is earlier.

Q.10. Describe the Evolution and Development of Banking system in India?

Ans. The evolution and development of the banking system in India can be traced back to ancient times when indigenous banking practices such as "Shroffs" and "Sahukars" operated as moneylenders and provided financial services to the local communities. However, the modern banking system in India began to take shape during the British colonial period.

Colonial Era: The establishment of the Bank of Bengal in 1806 marked the beginning of formal banking in India. Subsequently, the Bank of Bombay and the Bank of Madras were established in 1840. These three banks were later merged to form the Imperial Bank of India in 1921, which served as the precursor to the Reserve Bank of India (RBI).

Reserve Bank of India (RBI): The RBI was established in 1935 as the central banking authority responsible for regulating and supervising the banking sector in India. It was nationalized in 1949, giving the government significant control over monetary policy and banking operations.

Post-Independence Era: After India gained independence in 1947, the government initiated various reforms to promote financial inclusion and economic development. The nationalization of major banks in 1969 and 1980 aimed to expand banking services to rural areas and prioritize the needs of the marginalized sections of society.

Liberalization and Privatization: The 1991 economic reforms introduced liberalization and privatization measures, leading to the entry of private and foreign banks into the Indian banking sector. This resulted in increased competition, technological advancements, and improved customer services.

Digitalization and Financial Inclusion: In recent years, there has been a significant emphasis on digitalization and financial inclusion initiatives to expand access to banking services and promote cashless transactions across the country.

Overall, the evolution of the banking system in India reflects a dynamic journey from traditional practices to modern banking practices, driven by economic, political, and technological changes over time.

Q.11. Elucidate the salient features of FEMA.

Ans. The Foreign Exchange Management Act (FEMA) is a crucial legislation enacted in 1999 to consolidate and amend the law relating to foreign exchange with the objective of facilitating external trade and payments and promoting orderly development and maintenance of the foreign exchange market in India. The salient features of FEMA are:

Regulation of Foreign Exchange: FEMA regulates all aspects related to foreign exchange transactions, including dealings in foreign exchange, transfer of immovable property outside India, and acquisition and holding of foreign exchange.

Current and Capital Account Transactions: FEMA distinguishes between current account transactions (transactions related to trade, remittances, and personal expenses) and capital account transactions (investments, loans, and transfers of capital assets). It permits most current account transactions without restrictions while regulating capital account transactions.

Liberalization: FEMA introduced liberalization measures to simplify and rationalize foreign exchange regulations, thereby promoting ease of doing business and attracting foreign investment. It allows for greater flexibility in foreign exchange transactions and encourages foreign investment in various sectors of the economy.

Enforcement and Penalties: FEMA provides for stringent enforcement mechanisms and penalties for violations of its provisions, including penalties for contravention of foreign exchange regulations, unauthorized transactions, and non-compliance with reporting requirements.

Enforcement Directorate (ED): The ED is the designated enforcement agency responsible for investigating and prosecuting violations of FEMA. It has the authority to conduct inquiries, search premises, seize documents, and impose penalties.

Adjudication and Appeals: FEMA establishes adjudicating authorities to adjudicate on contraventions of its provisions and provides for appeals against their orders to the Appellate Tribunal for Foreign Exchange.

FEMA plays a crucial role in regulating foreign exchange transactions, promoting foreign investment, and maintaining stability in the Indian foreign exchange market. Its salient features reflect a balance between liberalization and regulatory oversight to facilitate international trade and investment while safeguarding the interests of the Indian economy.

Q.12. Describe the role of RBI in Indian Banking System.

Ans. The Reserve Bank of India (RBI) plays a central and multifaceted role in the Indian banking system, serving as the apex monetary authority and regulator. Its responsibilities encompass monetary policy formulation, banking regulation and supervision, currency issuance, management of foreign exchange reserves, and overall financial stability. The role of RBI in the Indian banking system can be elaborated as follows:

Monetary Policy Formulation: RBI formulates and implements monetary policy to achieve price stability and promote sustainable economic growth. It regulates key monetary variables such as money supply, interest rates, and inflation through various policy tools like repo rate, reverse repo rate, and open market operations.

Banking Regulation and Supervision: RBI regulates and supervises banks and financial institutions to ensure their solvency, soundness, and compliance with prudential norms and regulations. It issues guidelines on capital adequacy, asset quality, risk management, and corporate governance, conducts inspections, and takes corrective actions to maintain financial stability.

Currency Issuance and Management: RBI is responsible for the issuance, circulation, and management of currency in India. It ensures an adequate supply of currency notes and coins to meet the public's demand for cash and maintains the integrity and security of the currency.

Foreign Exchange Management: RBI manages India's foreign exchange reserves and formulates policies to promote external trade and payments. It regulates foreign exchange transactions, controls capital flows, and intervenes in the foreign exchange market to maintain exchange rate stability.

Developmental Functions: RBI undertakes various developmental initiatives to promote financial inclusion, enhance payment and settlement systems, and strengthen the banking infrastructure. It fosters innovation, supports banking technology upgrades, and encourages financial literacy and consumer protection.

In summary, RBI's pivotal role in the Indian banking system encompasses monetary policy formulation, banking regulation and supervision, currency management, foreign exchange control, and developmental functions aimed at maintaining financial stability and fostering inclusive and sustainable economic growth.

Q.13. Critically analyze the relationship between Bank & Customer.

Ans. The relationship between banks and customers is fundamental to the functioning of the banking system and the broader economy. It is characterized by a unique set of rights, obligations, and expectations for both parties.

On one hand, banks serve as financial intermediaries, providing a range of products and services to meet the diverse needs of customers. They offer deposit accounts, loans, investment products, and payment services, facilitating savings, investment, and consumption activities. Banks also play a critical role in allocating capital, mobilizing savings, and promoting economic growth through lending to businesses and individuals.

On the other hand, customers entrust their funds and financial transactions to banks, expecting reliability, security, and fair treatment in return. Customers rely on banks for safekeeping of their deposits, timely execution of transactions, access to credit, and professional financial advice. They also expect transparency, accountability, and protection of their rights as consumers.

However, the relationship between banks and customers is not without challenges and conflicts. Issues such as hidden fees, unfair practices, mis-selling of financial products, and breaches of customer privacy can erode trust and strain the relationship. Moreover, asymmetries in information and bargaining power often favor banks, leading to potential exploitation of customers.

To address these challenges and maintain a healthy relationship, it is essential for banks to prioritize customer interests, uphold ethical standards, and comply with regulatory requirements. Transparency, communication, and responsiveness to customer feedback are also crucial for building trust and fostering long-term relationships.

Similarly, customers must exercise diligence, prudence, and awareness of their rights and responsibilities while engaging with banks, thereby promoting mutual respect and accountability in the banking relationship.

Banking Law 2022 Question

Q.1. What is a garnishee order?

Ans. A garnishee order is a legal directive issued by a court that requires a third party, typically a bank or employer, to withhold funds from a debtor's account or salary to satisfy a debt owed to a creditor. The order compels the garnishee, the third party holding the debtor's assets, to transfer the specified amount directly to the creditor to settle the debt. Garnishee orders are often used in debt recovery proceedings when a debtor fails to repay a debt, providing creditors with a legal mechanism to recover funds owed to them.

Q.2. Dishonor of a bill of exchange by non-acceptance?

Ans. Dishonor of a bill of exchange by non-acceptance occurs when the drawee, upon presentation of the bill, refuses to accept it as valid or to acknowledge their obligation to pay. This refusal may be due to various reasons such as insufficient funds, discrepancy in the bill's terms, or the drawee's unwillingness to honor the payment. Non-acceptance results in the bill being dishonored, and the holder can take legal action against the drawer for breach of contract. It may also lead to additional penalties or legal consequences for the drawee, depending on the applicable laws and circumstances.

Q.3. Define 'payment in due course'?

Ans. Payment in due course refers to the lawful and timely settlement of a negotiable instrument, such as a bill of exchange or promissory note, by the party liable to make the payment. For a payment to be considered in due course, it must meet certain conditions: it must be made to the rightful holder of the instrument, in accordance with its terms, at the proper time, and without any irregularities or legal impediments. Payment in due course protects the payer from further liability and ensures the integrity and enforceability of negotiable instruments in commercial transactions.

Q.4. Parties to negotiable instruments ?

Ans. Under Indian law, parties to negotiable instruments include the drawer, who creates the instrument and orders payment; the drawee, who is directed to make the payment; and the payee, who is entitled to receive the payment. Additionally, there may be endorsers, who transfer their rights in the instrument to others, and endorsers-in-blank, who endorse the instrument without specifying the payee. These parties may be individuals, businesses, or financial institutions, and their roles and obligations are defined by the terms of the instrument and relevant provisions of the Negotiable Instruments Act, 1881.

Q.5. Describe the organizational structure of RBI.

Ans. The organizational structure of the Reserve Bank of India (RBI) comprises several key components. At the top is the Central Board of Directors, which provides overall direction and governance. The central board is supported by various committees and sub-committees. The RBI's operations are divided into several departments, including banking regulation and supervision, monetary policy, currency management, and economic research. Each department is headed by an executive director or deputy governor. The RBI also has regional offices across India, which oversee banking operations and implement central bank policies at the grassroots level. Overall, this hierarchical structure enables the RBI to effectively carry out its mandate of maintaining monetary stability and financial stability in the country.

Q.6. What are the salient features of the Foreign Exchange Management Act, 1998?

Ans. The Foreign Exchange Management Act (FEMA), 1999, is a significant legislation that regulates foreign exchange transactions in India. Some salient features of FEMA include:

Comprehensive Framework: FEMA provides a comprehensive legal framework for the management of foreign exchange transactions, replacing the erstwhile Foreign Exchange Regulation Act (FERA), 1973.

Liberalization of Regulations: FEMA reflects India's shift towards a more liberalized and market-oriented approach to foreign exchange management. It simplifies and rationalizes regulations governing foreign exchange transactions, facilitating easier cross-border trade and investment.

Focus on Current Account Transactions: FEMA distinguishes between current account transactions (trade in goods and services) and capital account transactions (investment and borrowing). It imposes fewer restrictions on current account transactions, promoting international trade and payments.

Enforcement Mechanisms: FEMA empowers the Reserve Bank of India (RBI) to regulate and enforce foreign exchange regulations, with stringent penalties for non-compliance. It also establishes special adjudication and appellate authorities to adjudicate disputes and violations.

FEMA plays a crucial role in facilitating India's integration into the global economy while ensuring prudent management of foreign exchange reserves and safeguarding against external vulnerabilities.

Q.7. Discuss the special relationship between a bank and its customer.

Ans. The relationship between a bank and its customer is characterized by a special legal and fiduciary duty owed by the bank to the customer. Some key aspects of this relationship include:

Fiduciary Duty: Banks owe a fiduciary duty to act in the best interests of their customers when handling their financial affairs. This duty requires banks to exercise the utmost care, honesty, and integrity in their dealings with customers.

Confidentiality: Banks are required to maintain strict confidentiality regarding their customers' financial information and transactions. They must ensure the privacy and security of customer data, only disclosing information in accordance with legal requirements or with the customer's consent.

Duty of Care: Banks have a duty of care to provide accurate and reliable financial services to their customers. This includes offering suitable financial products, providing accurate information, and safeguarding customer assets.

Duty to Inform: Banks have a duty to inform customers about the terms and conditions of their products and services, as well as any risks associated with them.

The special relationship between a bank and its customer is based on trust, confidence, and mutual obligations, with the bank acting as a trusted financial advisor and custodian of the customer's assets.

Q.8. Discuss the modes of crossing of a cheque and significance of non-negotiable crossing.

Ans. Crossing of a cheque refers to the process of drawing two parallel lines across the face of the cheque, along with certain instructions written between the lines. There are several modes of crossing a cheque, including:

General Crossing: When the words "and company" or "not negotiable" are written between the lines, it constitutes a general crossing. It directs the paying bank to only pay the cheque to a bank or financial institution, not to a specific individual or bearer.

Special Crossing: When the name of a specific bank is written between the lines, it constitutes a special crossing. It directs the paying bank to only pay the cheque to the specified bank.

The significance of non-negotiable crossing lies in enhancing the security and traceability of the cheque. It prevents the cheque from being cashed over the counter and restricts its negotiation to the banking system, reducing the risk of loss or fraud. Non-negotiable crossing provides an additional layer of protection for both the drawer and the payee against unauthorized or fraudulent encashment of the cheque.

Q.9. What is the legal status and functions of the Reserve Bank of India ? Discuss.

Ans. The Reserve Bank of India (RBI) holds a prominent position as the central bank of India, established under the Reserve Bank of India Act, 1934. It serves as the apex monetary authority responsible for regulating and supervising the country's banking and financial system. The legal status of the RBI is derived from its statutory authority conferred by the Reserve Bank of India Act, 1934, and other relevant legislations.

The functions of the Reserve Bank of India include:

Monetary Policy Formulation: The RBI formulates and implements monetary policy to achieve price stability, control inflation, and support sustainable economic growth. It manages key monetary policy instruments such as repo rate, reverse repo rate, and liquidity adjustment facility (LAF).

Banking Regulation and Supervision: The RBI regulates and supervises banks and financial institutions to maintain financial stability, safeguard depositors' interests, and ensure the soundness of the banking system. It issues licenses, sets prudential norms, and conducts inspections to monitor compliance with regulatory requirements.

Currency Management: The RBI has the exclusive authority to issue currency notes and coins in India, ensuring an adequate supply of currency to meet the needs of the economy.

Foreign Exchange Management: The RBI manages the country's foreign exchange reserves and regulates foreign exchange transactions to maintain external stability and support trade and investment flows.

The Reserve Bank of India plays a pivotal role in promoting monetary stability, financial sector development, and economic growth in India.

Q.10. What does dishonor of Cheque means? What are its kinds? What are the essentials for an action u/s 138 of negotiable instrument act.

Ans. Dishonor of a cheque refers to the refusal of the bank to honor the payment specified on the cheque presented for encashment. It occurs when the bank returns the cheque unpaid due to various reasons such as insufficient funds, irregular signature, post-dated cheque, account closed, or a stop-payment instruction.

There are two main kinds of dishonor of cheques:

Dishonor for Insufficient Funds: This occurs when there are insufficient funds available in the drawer's account to cover the amount mentioned on the cheque. It is one of the most common reasons for dishonor.

Dishonor for Other Reasons: Apart from insufficient funds, a cheque may be dishonored for reasons such as irregular signature, post-dated cheque, account closed, or a stop-payment instruction issued by the drawer.

For an action under Section 138 of the Negotiable Instruments Act, the following essentials must be fulfilled:

The cheque was issued towards discharge of a debt or liability.

The cheque was presented to the bank within a period of six months from the date it was drawn or within the validity period, whichever is earlier.

The cheque is returned unpaid by the bank due to insufficient funds or any other reason.

The payee serves a notice in writing within thirty days of the receipt of information from the bank regarding the dishonor of the cheque, demanding payment of the amount due.

The drawer fails to make payment of the amount within fifteen days of the receipt of the notice.

Q.11. Define indorsement and its kind. What will be the effect of forged indorsement? Discuss with relevant cases.

Ans. Indorsement, also spelled as endorsement, refers to the act of signing on the back of a negotiable instrument, such as a cheque or promissory note, to transfer or assign the rights to the instrument to another party. Indorsement serves as a mode of negotiation, enabling the transfer of ownership and entitlement to the instrument.

There are several types of indorsement, including:

Blank Indorsement: In a blank indorsement, the indorser simply signs their name on the back of the instrument without specifying a specific payee. The instrument becomes payable to the bearer, allowing it to be negotiated by delivery.

Special or Full Indorsement: In a special indorsement, the indorser specifies the name of the person to whom the instrument is to be payable. The instrument can only be negotiated to the specified person or their order.

Restrictive Indorsement: A restrictive indorsement limits the further negotiation or transfer of the instrument. Common restrictive indorsements include "For Deposit Only" or "Payee's Account Only."

The effect of a forged indorsement is that it renders the negotiation or transfer of the instrument invalid and may lead to legal consequences for the forger. In the case of forgery, the indorsement is considered void ab initio (from the beginning), and any subsequent transfers based on the forged indorsement are also invalidated.

A relevant case illustrating the effect of forged indorsement is "Laxmi Dhar & Ors. v. The Reserve Bank of India & Ors." In this case, the Supreme Court of India held that a forged indorsement does not confer any title or rights on the transferee, and the instrument remains the property of the rightful owner. The court emphasized the importance of ensuring the authenticity of indorsements to prevent fraud and protect the integrity of negotiable instruments.

Q.12. What do you understand by a 'Holder' and 'Holder in due course'? How do you distinguish between the two? Explain.

Ans. In the context of negotiable instruments like bills of exchange and promissory notes, a "holder" and a "holder in due course" refer to two distinct legal statuses that confer different rights and privileges.

A "holder" of a negotiable instrument is simply someone who is in possession of the instrument and is entitled to enforce it. This could be the original payee named on the instrument or any subsequent transferee who has acquired the instrument through proper endorsement or delivery. The holder has the right to demand payment of the instrument's amount from the party liable to pay.

On the other hand, a "holder in due course" is a special status conferred upon a holder who meets certain additional criteria specified in the law. To qualify as a holder in due course, the individual must:

Acquire the instrument for value: The holder must have given something of value (consideration) in exchange for the instrument.

Obtain the instrument in good faith: The holder must acquire the instrument without knowledge of any defects or irregularities, such as forgery, fraud, or outstanding claims or defenses against it.

Take the instrument without notice: The holder must acquire the instrument without notice of any facts that would make it invalid or unenforceable.

The main distinction between a holder and a holder in due course lies in their respective rights and privileges. While both holders can generally enforce the instrument, a holder in due course enjoys certain additional protections, such as immunity from certain defenses that could be raised against a regular holder, making their position stronger in legal disputes involving the instrument.

Q.13. What do you understand by collecting banker? Discuss the duties and functions of collecting bankers.

Ans. A collecting banker is a financial institution that collects and receives payment on behalf of its customers for instruments such as cheques, drafts, and other negotiable instruments. When a customer deposits such instruments into their bank account, the bank acts as a collecting banker, presenting the instruments to the drawee bank for payment and crediting the proceeds to the customer's account.

The duties and functions of a collecting banker include:

Collection of Instruments: The primary function of a collecting banker is to collect and receive payment for instruments deposited by customers into their accounts. This involves presenting the instruments to the drawee bank for payment and crediting the proceeds to the customer's account upon receipt.

Exercise of Due Diligence: A collecting banker must exercise due diligence in verifying the authenticity of the instruments presented for collection and ensuring compliance with legal requirements and banking procedures.

Provision of Collection Services: Collecting bankers offer collection services to their customers, including the collection of cheques, drafts, bills of exchange, and other negotiable instruments. They may also provide assistance and guidance to customers regarding the collection process.

Acting as an Agent: In the collection process, the collecting banker acts as an agent of the customer, collecting payment on their behalf. As such, the banker owes a duty of care to the customer to handle the collection process efficiently and accurately.

The duties and functions of a collecting banker revolve around facilitating the collection of funds on behalf of customers and ensuring the smooth operation of the collection process.

Banking Law 2018 Question Paper

Q.1. Define payment in due course.

Ans. Payment in due course refers to the payment of a negotiable instrument to a holder who has acquired it in good faith, for value, and without notice of any defects or irregularities that might invalidate the instrument. In other words, it is the payment made by the drawee or acceptor of a negotiable instrument in accordance with its terms and conditions, to a holder who has acquired the instrument legitimately. Payment in due course protects the rights of innocent holders who have taken the instrument in good faith and ensures the smooth functioning of negotiable instruments in commercial transactions.

Q.2. What are the main characteristics of Promissory note?

Ans. The main characteristics of a promissory note include:

Unconditional Promise: It contains an unconditional promise by the maker to pay a specified sum of money to the payee.

Signed by Maker: It must be signed by the maker, indicating their commitment to fulfill the promise.

Payee Designation: It specifies the person to whom the payment is to be made, known as the payee.

Fixed Amount: It states a fixed amount of money to be paid.

Payment Date: It may specify either a fixed date for payment or be payable on demand.

Legally Enforceable: It is legally binding and enforceable in court if not honored.

Q.3. What are Government Securities? Illustrate.

Ans. Government securities refer to debt instruments issued by the government to raise funds for financing its expenditures or managing its debt. These securities include treasury bills, government bonds, and government savings bonds. They are considered one of the safest investments as they are backed by the full faith and credit of the government. Investors purchase government securities for their low risk and steady income stream through interest payments or capital appreciation. Government securities play a crucial role in financial markets, serving as benchmarks for interest rates and providing liquidity and stability to the economy.

Q.4. Industrial Reconstruction Bank of India.

Ans. The Industrial Reconstruction Bank of India (IRBI) was a specialized financial institution established in 1971 to provide financial assistance for the rehabilitation and reconstruction of sick industrial units in India. Its primary objective was to revive and modernize financially distressed industrial enterprises through loans, debt restructuring, and technical assistance. IRBI played a crucial role in the industrial development of the country by supporting the revival of struggling industrial units, promoting employment generation, and contributing to economic growth. However, the bank was merged with the Industrial Development Bank of India (IDBI) in 1997 as part of a broader consolidation of financial institutions in India.

Q.5. Banking Company.

Ans. A banking company is a financial institution authorized by law to engage in banking activities, including accepting deposits, providing loans, and offering various financial services to customers. These services typically include savings and current accounts, credit facilities, investment services, and payment processing. Banking companies play a vital role in the economy by mobilizing savings, facilitating capital formation, and providing liquidity to businesses and individuals. They are subject to regulatory oversight and prudential norms to ensure stability, solvency, and consumer protection. Banking companies contribute to economic growth and development by intermediating funds between savers and borrowers, thereby promoting investment and entrepreneurship.

Q.6. Discuss briefly the different kinds of letters of credit. Which may be issued by a Bank?

Ans. Letters of credit are widely used in international trade to facilitate secure payment transactions between buyers and sellers. Different kinds of letters of credit include:

Revocable Letters of credit: Can be modified or canceled by the issuing bank without prior notice to the beneficiary.

Irrevocable Letters of credit: Cannot be modified or canceled without the consent of all parties involved.

Confirmed Letters of credit: Confirmed by a second bank (usually in the beneficiary's country) to provide additional assurance of payment.

Standby Letters of credit: Used as a backup payment method if the buyer fails to fulfill their obligations.

Transferable Letters of credit: Allows the beneficiary to transfer all or part of the LC proceeds to another party.

Back-to-Back Letters of credit: Used when the beneficiary needs to purchase goods from a supplier using the proceeds of the original LC.

Red Clause Letters of credit: Allows the beneficiary to receive an advance payment before shipping the goods.

Banks typically issue irrevocable, confirmed, standby, transferable, and back-to-back letters of credit, as these provide the highest level of security and flexibility in international trade transactions.

Q.7. Discuss the liabilities of a surety.

Ans. In banking, a surety is an individual or entity that provides a guarantee to a lender (usually a bank) for the repayment of a loan by a borrower. The liabilities of a surety in banking depend on the terms of the surety agreement and can be significant. Some of the key liabilities of a surety include:

Repayment Obligation: If the borrower defaults on the loan, the surety becomes liable to repay the outstanding debt to the lender. The surety is responsible for honoring the terms of the guarantee, including payment of the principal amount, accrued interest, and any associated costs or fees.

Legal Obligations: The surety may be subject to legal action by the lender to enforce the terms of the guarantee and recover the outstanding debt. This could involve court proceedings, judgments, and potential seizure of assets to satisfy the debt.

Credit Impact: A surety's creditworthiness and reputation may be adversely affected if they are required to fulfill the obligations of the guarantee. Defaulting on a surety obligation could lead to financial difficulties, damage to credit ratings, and challenges in obtaining future financing.

The liabilities of a surety in banking underscore the importance of careful consideration and assessment before providing a guarantee for a loan.

Q.8. What is meant by a 'Clearing House'. Explain its working.

Ans. A clearing house is a financial institution or intermediary that facilitates the settlement of financial transactions between multiple parties, typically banks or other financial institutions. Its primary function is to centralize and streamline the process of clearing and settling payments, securities, and other financial instruments.

The working of a clearing house involves several steps:

Receipt of Transactions: Banks and financial institutions submit transactions, such as checks, electronic transfers, or securities trades, to the clearing house for processing.

Verification and Matching: The clearing house verifies the details of each transaction, including the authenticity of the instruments and the availability of funds.

Netting: The clearing house aggregates transactions between participating institutions and calculates net positions to minimize the number of actual payments required.

Settlement: Funds or securities are transferred between accounts held at the clearing house to settle the net obligations of participating institutions.

Reporting: The clearing house provides reports to participating institutions detailing the status of transactions, including any discrepancies or exceptions.

Overall, a clearing house enhances the efficiency, reliability, and safety of financial transactions by providing a centralized platform for the clearing and settlement process, thereby reducing risk and facilitating smoother transactions between counterparties.

Q.9. Discuss briefly the legal status and functions of the Reserve Bank of India. In what manner Reserve Bank may control the process of Inflation and price rise in the economy?

Ans. The Reserve Bank of India (RBI) is the central bank of India and is endowed with various legal powers and functions to regulate the country's monetary and financial system. It operates under the Reserve Bank of India Act, 1934, and its functions are broadly categorized into:

Monetary Policy: The RBI formulates and implements monetary policy to achieve price stability and economic growth. It uses tools such as interest rates, open market operations, reserve requirements, and liquidity management to control the money supply and credit conditions in the economy.

Currency Issuance: The RBI has the sole authority to issue currency notes and coins in India, ensuring an adequate and stable supply of currency to meet the needs of the economy.

Banking Regulation: The RBI regulates and supervises banks and financial institutions to maintain the stability and integrity of the banking system. It issues licenses, sets prudential norms, conducts inspections, and takes corrective actions to address risks and ensure compliance with regulatory requirements.

Foreign Exchange Management: The RBI manages the country's foreign exchange reserves and regulates foreign exchange transactions to maintain external stability and support trade and investment flows.

To control inflation and price rise in the economy, the RBI employs various monetary policy measures. For instance, during periods of inflationary pressures, the RBI may raise interest rates to reduce demand and curb inflation. It may also conduct open market operations to sell government securities, thereby draining excess liquidity from the financial system. Additionally, the RBI may increase reserve requirements for banks, restricting their ability to lend and spend, thereby reducing inflationary pressures in the economy. Through these measures, the RBI aims to stabilize prices and maintain economic stability.

Q.10. Define 'Bill of Exchange'. What are the characteristics? Describe the different kinds of Bills of Exchange.

Ans. A bill of exchange is a negotiable instrument that contains an unconditional written order from one party (the drawer) to another party (the drawee) directing the drawee to pay a specified sum of money to a third party (the payee) either immediately or at a future date. It serves as a legally binding document that facilitates commercial transactions and payment obligations between parties.

Characteristics of a bill of exchange include:

Unconditional Order: The order to pay contained in the bill of exchange must be unconditional, meaning it is not subject to any conditions or contingencies.

Three Parties: A bill of exchange involves three parties: the drawer who issues the order, the drawee who is directed to make the payment, and the payee who is entitled to receive the payment.

Payment Obligation: The drawee is legally obligated to make the payment specified in the bill of exchange to the payee.

Negotiability: Bills of exchange are negotiable instruments, meaning they can be freely transferred or negotiated to a third party, thereby facilitating the transfer of debt or payment obligations.

There are several kinds of bills of exchange, including:

Trade Bill: Used in commercial transactions to facilitate payment for goods or services.

Accommodation Bill: Drawn and accepted without any consideration or underlying transaction, often used for credit arrangements.

Documentary Bill: Supported by shipping documents or other trade-related documents to evidence the underlying transaction.

Inland Bill: Drawn and payable within the same country.

Foreign Bill: Drawn and payable in different countries, involving international trade transactions.

These different kinds of bills of exchange cater to various commercial and financial needs, providing flexibility and efficiency in payment transactions.

Q.11. The basic law regarding formation and regulation of Banking Companies in India is contained in the Banking Companies Act 1949 and the Banking Regulation Act 1949. Outline briefly the main features of these two acts.

Ans. The Banking Companies Act, 1949, and the Banking Regulation Act, 1949, are two key pieces of legislation governing the formation and regulation of banking companies in India. Here are the main features of these two acts:

Banking Companies Act, 1949:

The Banking Companies Act, 1949, provides for the regulation and supervision of banking companies in India.

It defines the term "banking company" and lays down the requirements for the formation, incorporation, and registration of banking companies.

The act sets out the various provisions related to the management, administration, and operations of banking companies, including provisions regarding share capital, management structure, and powers of the board of directors.

It outlines the regulatory framework for the functioning of banking companies, including provisions related to licensing, restrictions on banking activities, and regulatory oversight by the Reserve Bank of India (RBI).

The act also contains provisions related to amalgamation, reconstruction, and winding up of banking companies, as well as provisions related to penalties for non-compliance with the provisions of the act.

Banking Regulation Act, 1949:

The Banking Regulation Act, 1949, is a comprehensive legislation that provides for the regulation and supervision of banking companies in India.

It empowers the Reserve Bank of India (RBI) to regulate and supervise banking companies in matters related to licensing, management, operations, and financial stability.

The act lays down the regulatory framework for various aspects of banking operations, including capital adequacy, liquidity management, lending practices, and asset quality.

It establishes the legal framework for the establishment of branches, subsidiaries, and representative offices by banking companies.

The act also provides for the inspection, audit, and reporting requirements for banking companies, as well as provisions related to penalties for non-compliance with the regulatory requirements.

The Banking Companies Act, 1949, and the Banking Regulation Act, 1949, together form the core legal framework for the regulation and supervision of banking companies in India, ensuring stability, integrity, and efficiency in the banking sector.

Q.12. What is priority lending? Discuss.

Ans. Priority lending refers to the practice of directing a certain proportion of a bank's lending activities towards specific sectors or segments of the economy that are deemed important for socio-economic development. It is a regulatory requirement imposed by central banks or government authorities to ensure that financial resources are allocated towards priority areas that contribute to inclusive growth, poverty alleviation, and balanced regional development.

In India, priority lending targets sectors such as agriculture, micro, small, and medium enterprises (MSMEs), education, housing, and export credit, among others. Banks are mandated to allocate a certain percentage of their total lending portfolio towards these priority sectors, as prescribed by the Reserve Bank of India (RBI) through its priority sector lending guidelines.

Priority lending serves several purposes:

Promoting Inclusive Growth: By channeling credit to underserved and marginalized sectors of society, priority lending helps promote inclusive growth and reduce socio-economic disparities.

Supporting Key Sectors: It provides critical financial support to sectors such as agriculture and MSMEs, which are vital for employment generation, rural development, and economic resilience.

Meeting Policy Objectives: Priority lending aligns with government policy objectives related to poverty alleviation, rural development, infrastructure investment, and sustainable development goals.

Strengthening Financial Inclusion: It encourages banks to extend banking services to underserved areas and population segments, thereby promoting financial inclusion and access to credit.

Priority lending is an important policy tool to ensure that the benefits of financial services reach all sections of society and contribute to sustainable and inclusive economic growth.

Q.13. What do you mean by a 'Holder' and 'Holder in due course'? How do you distinguish between the two? Explain.

Ans. In the context of negotiable instruments like bills of exchange and promissory notes, a "holder" and a "holder in due course" refer to two different legal statuses that affect the rights and liabilities associated with the instrument.

A "holder" is simply someone who is in possession of a negotiable instrument and is entitled to enforce it. This could be the original payee or any subsequent transferee who has acquired the instrument through proper endorsement or delivery.

On the other hand, a "holder in due course" is a special status conferred upon a holder who meets certain additional criteria specified in the law. To qualify as a holder in due course, the individual must:

Acquire the instrument for value: The holder must have given something of value (consideration) in exchange for the instrument.

Obtain the instrument in good faith: The holder must acquire the instrument without knowledge of any defects or irregularities, such as forgery, fraud, or outstanding claims or defenses against it.

Take the instrument without notice: The holder must acquire the instrument without notice of any facts that would make it invalid or unenforceable.

The main distinction between a holder and a holder in due course lies in their respective rights and privileges. While both holders can generally enforce the instrument, a holder in due course enjoys certain additional protections, such as immunity from certain defenses that could be raised against a regular holder, making their position stronger in legal disputes involving the instrument.

Banking Law 2017 Question Paper

Q.1. Promissory Note.

Ans. A promissory note is a written, unconditional, and signed financial instrument containing a promise by one party (the maker or issuer) to pay a specified sum of money to another party (the payee) at a predetermined future date or on demand. It serves as evidence of a debt obligation and outlines the terms of repayment, including the principal amount, interest rate (if any), maturity date, and any other relevant terms and conditions. Promissory notes are commonly used in commercial transactions, loans, and financing arrangements as a formal acknowledgment of debt and a commitment to repay the borrowed funds.

Q.2. Lost Instrument.

Ans. In the context of the Negotiable Instruments Act, a lost instrument refers to a negotiable instrument, such as a promissory note or bill of exchange, which has been misplaced, stolen, or destroyed. When a negotiable instrument is lost, the person who was entitled to it may apply to the court for a duplicate instrument, provided they can prove the loss and give a sufficient indemnity to protect the rights of other parties involved. The court may issue a duplicate instrument upon being satisfied with the applicant's evidence and indemnity, ensuring that the rights of all parties are safeguarded in the transaction.

Q.3. Letter of credit.

Ans. A letter of credit is a financial instrument issued by a bank on behalf of a buyer, promising to pay the seller a specified amount of money upon the presentation of certain documents and compliance with predetermined terms and conditions. It serves as a guarantee of payment for the seller, ensuring that they will receive payment for goods or services provided to the buyer. Letters of credit are commonly used in international trade transactions to mitigate payment risks and facilitate smooth transactions between buyers and sellers located in different countries. They provide security and confidence to both parties involved in the transaction.

Q.4. Banking Company.

Ans. A banking company is a financial institution authorized by law to engage in banking activities such as accepting deposits, granting loans, and providing various financial services to customers. These services typically include deposit accounts, credit facilities, investment services, and payment processing. Banking companies play a crucial role in the economy by mobilizing savings, facilitating capital formation, and providing liquidity to businesses and individuals. They are regulated by banking laws and overseen by regulatory authorities to ensure compliance with prudential norms, consumer protection, and financial stability. Banking companies are essential pillars of the financial system, contributing to economic growth and development.

Q.5. Reserve Bank of India.

Ans. The Reserve Bank of India (RBI) is India's central bank, responsible for formulating and implementing monetary policy, regulating and supervising the banking sector, and managing the country's currency and foreign exchange reserves. Established in 1935, the RBI serves as the apex financial institution, tasked with maintaining price stability, promoting economic growth, and ensuring the stability of the financial system. It issues currency, regulates and licenses banks, manages government debt, and acts as the banker and debt manager to the central and state governments. The RBI plays a crucial role in India's financial and economic landscape, guiding monetary policy decisions and maintaining financial stability.

Q.6. Define and differentiate between 'Holder' & 'Holder in due course'.

Ans. Under the banking law, a "holder" refers to any person who is in possession of a negotiable instrument, such as a promissory note or bill of exchange, and is entitled to enforce it in their own name. The holder may have obtained the instrument through various means, such as by purchase, gift, or endorsement.

On the other hand, a "holder in due course" is a special category of holder who meets specific requirements under the law. To be considered an Holder in due course, the holder must have acquired the negotiable instrument for value, in good faith, and without notice of any defects or irregularities in the instrument. An holder in due course enjoys certain legal advantages, including the ability to enforce the instrument free from certain defenses and claims that may be raised against the original parties to the instrument.

In summary, while both a holder and a holder in due course possess a negotiable instrument, an Holder in due course holds a superior legal position due to the specific requirements they must meet under the law.

Q.7. Discuss the special services provided by banks.

Ans. Banks provide a range of special services to enhance the banking experience and meet the diverse needs of their customers. These services include:

Online and Mobile Banking: Convenient platforms allow customers to manage their accounts, transfer funds, pay bills, and access banking services anytime, anywhere.

Personalized Financial Advice: Banks offer financial planning and advisory services to help customers achieve their financial goals, whether it's saving for retirement, buying a home, or planning for education.

Rewards Programs: Many banks offer rewards programs that allow customers to earn points or cashback on their purchases, incentivizing the use of banking products and services.

Loan Products: Banks provide various loan products, including personal loans, home loans, and auto loans, with competitive interest rates and flexible repayment terms.

Investment Services: Banks offer investment products such as mutual funds, stocks, bonds, and retirement accounts to help customers grow their wealth and achieve long-term financial security.

Insurance Services: Banks provide insurance products such as life insurance, health insurance, and property insurance to protect customers and their assets against unforeseen events.

Concierge Services: Some banks offer concierge services to assist customers with travel bookings, event planning, and other lifestyle-related needs.

These special services cater to the individual preferences and financial objectives of customers, enhancing their banking experience and fostering long-term relationships with the bank.

Q.8. What do you mean by 'Bill of Exchange'?

Ans. A bill of exchange is a negotiable instrument that serves as a written order issued by one party (the drawer) to another party (the drawee) directing the drawee to pay a specified sum of money to a third party (the payee) either immediately or at a future date. It is commonly used in commercial transactions as a means of facilitating payment for goods or services provided.

A bill of exchange typically contains essential elements, including the names of the parties involved, the amount of money to be paid, the date and place of payment, and the signature of the drawer. It is a legally binding document that creates a contractual obligation for the drawee to make payment to the payee according to the terms specified in the bill.

Bills of exchange are governed by the provisions of the Negotiable Instruments Act, 1881, and are widely used in domestic and international trade as a secure and efficient method of payment and credit extension.

Q.9. What do you mean by a Secured Loan? What are the modes of Securing a loan by a bank?

Ans. A secured loan refers to a type of loan that is backed by collateral provided by the borrower. Collateral is an asset or property that the borrower pledges to the lender to secure the loan, thereby reducing the lender's risk of default. In the event that the borrower fails to repay the loan according to the terms of the agreement, the lender has the right to seize and sell the collateral to recover the outstanding debt.

There are several modes of securing a loan by a bank:

Real Estate Mortgage: This involves using real property, such as land or buildings, as collateral for the loan. The bank holds a mortgage or deed of trust on the property until the loan is fully repaid.

Vehicle Collateral: Borrowers may pledge their vehicles, such as cars, trucks, or motorcycles, as collateral for the loan. The bank holds the vehicle title until the loan is paid off.

Pledge of Marketable Securities: Borrowers can pledge marketable securities, such as stocks, bonds, or mutual funds, as collateral for the loan. The bank holds the securities until the loan is satisfied.

Deposit Collateral: Some banks offer secured loans where the borrower's savings account, certificate of deposit (CD), or other deposit accounts are used as collateral for the loan. The funds in the account serve as security for the loan amount.

Personal Property: Borrowers may also pledge personal property, such as jewelry, art, or valuable collectibles, as collateral for the loan. The bank may hold possession of the property until the loan is repaid.

These modes of securing a loan provide lenders with assurance and mitigate the risk of default, allowing them to offer borrowers more favorable terms and lower interest rates compared to unsecured loans.

Q.10. Discuss the liability of a surety..

Ans. In banking law, a surety is a person who agrees to be responsible for the debt or obligation of another party (the principal debtor) in the event of default. The liability of a surety is significant and carries legal consequences under the terms of the surety agreement.

Primary Liability: A surety's liability is secondary to that of the principal debtor, meaning the surety is obligated to fulfill the debt or obligation only if the principal debtor fails to do so. However, once the principal debtor defaults, the surety becomes primarily liable for the debt, and the creditor can seek repayment directly from the surety.

Joint and Several Liability: In some cases, the surety may be held jointly and severally liable with the principal debtor, meaning the creditor has the option to pursue either party for the full amount of the debt. This increases the surety's risk exposure and potential liability.

Limited Liability: The liability of a surety may be limited to a specific amount or time period as stipulated in the surety agreement. If the surety's liability is limited, they are only responsible for the agreed-upon amount or duration of the obligation.

Indemnification: In the event that the surety is required to fulfill the obligation on behalf of the principal debtor, the surety may seek indemnification from the principal debtor for any losses or expenses incurred as a result.

The liability of a surety in banking law is significant and involves assuming responsibility for the debt or obligation of another party, with potential legal and financial consequences for the surety.

Q.11. Define endorsement. Discuss various types of endorsement with illustration.

Ans. Endorsement in the context of the Negotiable Instruments Act refers to the act of signing or endorsing a negotiable instrument, such as a promissory note or bill of exchange, to transfer or assign rights to another party. It serves as a method of negotiation, allowing the instrument to be freely transferred from one person to another.

There are several types of endorsements recognized under the Negotiable Instruments Act:

Blank Endorsement: In a blank endorsement, the endorser simply signs their name on the back of the instrument without specifying a particular endorsee. This transforms the instrument into a bearer instrument, which can be negotiated by mere delivery.

Special or Full Endorsement: A special or full endorsement specifies the person to whom or to whose order the instrument is payable. It typically includes the phrase "pay to the order of [name]" followed by the endorser's signature. This type of endorsement restricts further negotiation to the specified endorsee.

Restrictive Endorsement: A restrictive endorsement places conditions or restrictions on the further negotiation or use of the instrument. For example, an endorsement stating "For deposit only" limits the instrument to deposit into the specified endorsee's account.

Partial Endorsement: A partial endorsement involves endorsing only a part of the instrument, such as a specific amount, leaving the remaining portion payable to the original payee.

Qualified Endorsement: A qualified endorsement limits the endorser's liability on the instrument, typically by adding the phrase "without recourse" or similar language to the endorsement.

Each type of endorsement serves different purposes and has varying legal implications, providing flexibility in the negotiation and transfer of negotiable instruments.

Q.12. Discuss the functions of the Reserve Bank of India?

Ans. The Reserve Bank of India (RBI) serves as the central bank of India and performs a variety of functions to regulate and supervise the country's banking and financial system, formulate and implement monetary policy, and maintain financial stability. Some of the key functions of the RBI are as follows:

Monetary Policy Formulation: The RBI formulates and implements monetary policy to achieve the objectives of price stability, economic growth, and financial stability. It uses various monetary tools such as interest rates, open market operations, and reserve requirements to regulate money supply and credit in the economy.

Currency Issuance and Management: The RBI has the sole authority to issue currency notes and coins in India. It manages the supply, distribution, and withdrawal of currency to ensure the availability of an adequate and secure currency supply.

Banking Regulation and Supervision: The RBI regulates and supervises banks and financial institutions to maintain the stability and integrity of the banking system. It issues licenses, sets prudential norms, conducts inspections, and takes corrective actions to address risks and ensure compliance with regulatory requirements.

Foreign Exchange Management: The RBI manages the country's foreign exchange reserves and regulates foreign exchange transactions to maintain external stability and support trade and investment flows.

Developmental Functions: The RBI undertakes various developmental initiatives to promote financial inclusion, enhance payment and settlement systems, and foster innovation and efficiency in the financial sector.

Government Debt Management: The RBI acts as the banker to the central and state governments, managing their public debt issuance, servicing, and redemption.

Financial Stability Oversight: The RBI monitors and assesses risks to financial stability, takes proactive measures to address systemic risks, and coordinates with other regulatory agencies to safeguard the stability of the financial system.

The RBI plays a crucial role in maintaining monetary stability, promoting financial sector development, and ensuring the smooth functioning of the Indian economy.

Q.13. Discuss the meaning and kinds of Negotiable Instruments.

Ans. Negotiable instruments are documents that represent a right to payment of money and are freely transferable from one party to another. These instruments serve as a substitute for money and facilitate commercial transactions by providing a convenient and secure means of payment. The Negotiable Instruments Act, 1881 in India governs the law relating to negotiable instruments.

There are three main kinds of negotiable instruments:

Promissory Notes: A promissory note is a written promise made by one party (the maker) to pay a specified sum of money to another party (the payee) either on demand or at a fixed future date. It contains an unconditional promise to pay and is signed by the maker. Promissory notes are commonly used in personal loans, credit transactions, and financing arrangements.

Bills of Exchange: A bill of exchange is an unconditional written order made by one party (the drawer) to another party (the drawee) directing the drawee to pay a specified sum of money to a third party (the payee) either immediately or at a future date. Bills of exchange are used primarily in commercial transactions, such as the sale of goods or services, and facilitate credit transactions between parties.

Cheques: A cheque is a written order issued by an account holder (the drawer) to their bank (the drawee) directing the bank to pay a specified sum of money to the bearer or a named payee. Cheques are widely used for making payments, transferring funds, and settling debts in both personal and commercial transactions.

These negotiable instruments serve as important instruments in commerce and finance, providing flexibility, convenience, and security in conducting transactions. They are subject to specific legal requirements and protections under the law to ensure their validity, enforceability, and negotiability.

CHAPTER FIVE

Alternative Dispute Resolution & ADR's

ADR 2023 Question Paper

Q.1. Define Legal Representative.

Ans. A legal representative under the Arbitration and Conciliation Act refers to an individual or entity authorized to represent a party in arbitration proceedings. This representative may be an advocate, lawyer, or any other person duly authorized to act on behalf of the party in legal matters. The legal representative has the authority to make submissions, present evidence, cross-examine witnesses, and conduct negotiations on behalf of the party they represent. They play a crucial role in advocating for the party's interests and ensuring effective representation throughout the arbitration process.

Q.2. What is the nature of the ADR system?

Ans. The nature of Alternative Dispute Resolution (ADR) system is primarily consensual, flexible, and informal. It provides parties with an alternative avenue to resolve disputes outside of traditional court litigation. ADR methods such as mediation, arbitration, and negotiation allow parties to maintain control over the resolution process, tailor solutions to their specific needs, and preserve relationships. ADR emphasizes confidentiality, efficiency, and cost-effectiveness, offering parties a faster and less adversarial means of resolving conflicts. It promotes cooperation, creativity, and mutual respect, fostering outcomes that are acceptable and satisfactory to all parties involved.

Q.3. Who is entitled for legal services?

Ans. Legal services are typically available to individuals who require assistance with legal matters but cannot afford to hire private lawyers. Those entitled to legal services often include low-income individuals, marginalized communities, victims of discrimination or abuse, and individuals facing criminal charges without adequate representation. Legal aid organizations, pro bono lawyers, and government-funded programs often provide legal services to eligible individuals, ensuring access to justice and equality before the law. The entitlement to legal services is based on principles of fairness, equality, and the right to a fair trial, as enshrined in domestic and international legal frameworks.

Q.4. What do you mean by domestic arbitration?

Ans. Domestic arbitration refers to the resolution of disputes through arbitration proceedings conducted within the borders of a single country. It involves parties from the same jurisdiction who have agreed to resolve their disputes outside of the traditional court system. Domestic arbitration may be governed by the laws and regulations of the country where the arbitration takes place. It offers parties a private and neutral forum to resolve their disputes, typically faster and more cost-effective than traditional litigation. Domestic arbitration awards are enforceable within the jurisdiction where they are rendered, providing parties with a final and binding resolution to their disputes.

Q.5. Define Jurisdiction.

Ans. Jurisdiction under the Arbitration and Conciliation Act refers to the authority or power of a particular arbitral tribunal to hear and decide a dispute. It encompasses the scope of matters that the tribunal is competent to adjudicate upon, as well as the geographic and temporal limitations of its authority. Jurisdiction may be determined by the arbitration agreement between the parties, the law governing the arbitration, and any applicable rules or regulations. The Act sets forth provisions regarding the jurisdiction of arbitral tribunals, ensuring that disputes are resolved within the parameters established by the parties and the law.

Q.6. Discuss the conciliation settlement agreement.

Ans. A conciliation settlement agreement is a crucial outcome of the conciliation process, where parties to a dispute voluntarily reach a mutually acceptable resolution with the assistance of a neutral third party known as a conciliator. This agreement is a formal document that outlines the terms and conditions agreed upon by the parties to resolve their dispute amicably.

The conciliation settlement agreement typically includes details such as the agreed-upon settlement amount, specific actions or obligations each party must undertake, timelines for fulfilling those obligations, and any other relevant terms and conditions. It is binding upon the parties and serves as a legally enforceable contract once signed.

The agreement is drafted with the intention of providing a comprehensive and clear framework for the resolution of the dispute, ensuring that all parties understand their rights and responsibilities. Additionally, the conciliation settlement agreement often includes provisions for the termination of the conciliation proceedings and the dismissal of any related legal actions or claims.

Overall, the conciliation settlement agreement represents a consensual and final resolution to the dispute, reflecting the parties' willingness to cooperate and move forward without the need for further litigation or arbitration.

Q.7. 'Lok Adalat is a synonym of cheap and speedy justice'. What steps should be taken to make these adalats more effective?

Ans. To enhance the effectiveness of Lok Adalats and further reinforce their reputation as vehicles for cheap and speedy justice, several steps can be taken:

Awareness Campaigns: Conducting extensive awareness campaigns to educate the general public about the benefits and procedures of Lok Adalats. This includes disseminating information through various mediums such as print, electronic media, social media, and community outreach programs.

Strengthening Infrastructure: Investing in the infrastructure and facilities of Lok Adalat centers to ensure they are adequately equipped to handle a large number of cases efficiently. This includes providing sufficient space, technology, and personnel to facilitate the proceedings.

Training and Capacity Building: Offering regular training and capacity-building programs for the staff, including judges, lawyers, and support personnel involved in Lok Adalat proceedings. This ensures they are well-equipped with the necessary skills and knowledge to effectively administer justice through alternative dispute resolution mechanisms.

Promoting Mediation and Negotiation Skills: Emphasizing the importance of mediation and negotiation skills among the conciliators and parties involved in Lok Adalat proceedings. Encouraging parties to actively participate in the resolution process and explore amicable solutions to their disputes.

Simplification of Procedures: Streamlining and simplifying the procedures for referring cases to Lok Adalats, including the documentation and paperwork required. This reduces administrative burdens and ensures a more seamless and efficient resolution process.

Incentives and Recognition: Introducing incentives and recognition programs to motivate stakeholders, including judges, lawyers, and parties, to actively participate in Lok Adalat proceedings. This may include awards, honors, or other forms of recognition for outstanding contributions to the success of Lok Adalats.

Monitoring and Evaluation: Establishing robust monitoring and evaluation mechanisms to track the performance and outcomes of Lok Adalats. This enables continuous improvement and identifies areas for intervention or enhancement to maximize their effectiveness in delivering cheap and speedy justice to the masses.

ADR 2022 Question Paper

Q.1. Domestic Award.

Ans. A domestic award refers to a decision or judgment rendered by an arbitral tribunal in a domestic arbitration proceeding. It is issued following the resolution of a dispute between parties within the jurisdiction of a single country, in accordance with the applicable arbitration laws and procedures. The domestic award typically sets out the tribunal's findings on the merits of the case, any relief granted to the parties, and the reasoning behind the decision. Once issued, a domestic award is legally binding on the parties involved and can be enforced through the courts of the relevant jurisdiction.

Q.2. Fast Track Arbitration.

Ans. Fast-track arbitration is a streamlined and expedited arbitration process designed to resolve disputes swiftly and efficiently. It typically involves simplified procedures, limited documentary evidence, shorter timelines for hearings, and expedited decision-making by the arbitral tribunal. The aim of fast-track arbitration is to reduce costs, save time, and provide parties with a quicker resolution to their disputes compared to traditional arbitration proceedings. It is often used for less complex cases where parties seek a rapid and cost-effective resolution without compromising fairness or due process.

Q.3. International Commercial Arbitration.

Ans. International commercial arbitration is a widely recognized method for resolving cross-border commercial disputes outside the traditional court system. It involves parties from different countries agreeing to submit their dispute to arbitration, usually governed by international arbitration rules such as those of the ICC or UNCITRAL. International arbitration offers parties flexibility, neutrality, and enforceability of awards across multiple jurisdictions through the New York Convention. It promotes efficiency and confidentiality in resolving complex international disputes, providing parties with a forum to tailor proceedings to their specific needs and preferences while ensuring impartial adjudication by experienced arbitrators.

Q.4. Conciliator.

Ans. A conciliator is a neutral third party appointed to facilitate the resolution of disputes between parties through the process of conciliation. Unlike an arbitrator who renders a binding decision, a conciliator assists parties in reaching a mutually acceptable settlement voluntarily. The conciliator guides the parties through open communication, assists in identifying common interests, facilitates negotiation, and helps generate creative solutions to the issues in dispute. Their role involves fostering cooperation, maintaining impartiality, and encouraging parties to explore constructive dialogue to achieve a mutually beneficial outcome while preserving relationships.

Q.5. Necessary requisites for appointment of Arbitration.

Ans. The necessary requisites for the appointment of arbitration typically include:

Arbitration Agreement: A valid and enforceable arbitration agreement between the parties, either in the form of a standalone contract clause or a separate agreement.

Selection of Arbitrator(s): Agreement on the method and process for appointing the arbitrator(s), which may involve mutual consent, nomination by a designated authority, or selection from a pre-agreed list of arbitrators.

Qualifications: Ensuring that the appointed arbitrator(s) possess the necessary qualifications, expertise, and impartiality to fairly adjudicate the dispute.

Compliance with Legal Requirements: Adherence to any legal requirements or procedural formalities prescribed under applicable arbitration laws or rules governing the arbitration process.

Q.6. Finality of the 'Arbitral Award'

Ans. The finality of an arbitral award is a fundamental aspect of arbitration, signifying the conclusive nature of the decision rendered by the arbitral tribunal. Once an arbitral tribunal issues its award, it is considered final and binding upon the parties involved in the dispute. This means that the parties are generally precluded from challenging the merits of the decision before national courts, except in limited circumstances provided for by the applicable arbitration law or agreed upon by the parties. The finality of the arbitral award promotes the swift and efficient resolution of disputes, enhances the enforceability of the decision, and fosters confidence in the arbitration process. It also reflects the principle of party autonomy, whereby parties have the freedom to resolve their disputes through arbitration and abide by the outcome reached by the arbitral tribunal. Overall, the finality of the arbitral award is a cornerstone of arbitration, contributing to its effectiveness as an alternative dispute resolution mechanism.

Q.7. Difference between arbitration and conciliation.

Ans. Arbitration and conciliation are both alternative dispute resolution methods, but they differ in key aspects:

Decision-Making Authority: In arbitration, the arbitrator(s) render a binding decision known as an arbitral award after hearing arguments and evidence from the parties. The award is enforceable like a court judgment. In contrast, a conciliator facilitates negotiation between parties and assists them in reaching a mutually acceptable settlement. The conciliator does not impose a decision but helps parties find common ground.

Role of the Neutral Third Party: In arbitration, the arbitrator acts as a judge, applying the law and making a final determination on the dispute. In conciliation, the conciliator serves as a mediator, guiding discussions, fostering communication, and helping parties explore solutions.

Legal Formality: Arbitration proceedings follow formal rules and procedures, akin to litigation, with evidentiary hearings and legal submissions. Conciliation, on the other hand, is less formal, allowing for more flexible and creative problem-solving approaches.

Both methods aim to resolve disputes outside of court, arbitration results in a binding decision rendered by an arbitrator, whereas conciliation focuses on facilitating negotiations for a mutually agreeable settlement with the assistance of a conciliator.

Q.8. What is the importance of 'Arbitration clause' in a contract deed.

Ans. An arbitration clause in a contract deed is of significant importance as it serves several crucial purposes:

Dispute Resolution Mechanism: It provides a predetermined method for resolving disputes that may arise between the parties to the contract. By specifying arbitration as the preferred method of dispute resolution, the parties avoid potentially lengthy and costly litigation in court.

Party Autonomy: The inclusion of an arbitration clause allows parties to tailor the arbitration process to their specific needs and preferences. They can select the arbitral tribunal, choose the applicable law, and determine procedural rules, thereby maintaining a degree of control over the resolution process.

Enforcement and Finality: Arbitration awards are generally easier to enforce across borders than court judgments due to international conventions such as the New York Convention. The arbitration process also offers finality, as arbitral awards are typically binding and not subject to appeal.

An arbitration clause promotes efficiency, predictability, and flexibility in dispute resolution, contributing to the smooth functioning of contractual relationships.

Q.9. Discuss the meaning and field of 'Alternate Dispute Resolution System'. Also discuss its importance.

Ans. Alternative Dispute Resolution (ADR) refers to a range of mechanisms for resolving disputes outside of traditional court litigation. It includes methods such as arbitration, mediation, negotiation, conciliation, and collaborative law. ADR provides parties with flexible and informal processes to resolve conflicts more efficiently, cost-effectively, and amicably.

The field of ADR encompasses various sectors, including commercial disputes, family law matters, labor and employment disputes, construction disputes, and community disputes. It is widely used in business transactions, international commerce, consumer disputes, and interpersonal conflicts.

The importance of ADR lies in its ability to offer parties more control over the resolution process, greater confidentiality, faster outcomes, and reduced costs compared to litigation. ADR promotes cooperation, communication, and creative problem-solving, leading to mutually acceptable solutions and preserving relationships between parties. It also helps alleviate the burden on court systems by diverting cases away from overcrowded dockets, thus contributing to the efficient administration of justice. Overall, ADR plays a vital role in promoting access to justice, fostering trust in legal systems, and promoting peaceful dispute resolution in diverse contexts.

Q.10. Trace the history of 'Legal Aid' citing laws pertaining to 'legal aid'

Ans. The concept of legal aid, which aims to ensure equal access to justice regardless of one's financial means, has a rich historical evolution spanning centuries:

Magna Carta (1215): While not explicitly related to legal aid, the Magna Carta laid the groundwork for principles of due process and access to justice, which are foundational to the concept of legal aid.

Legal Aid and Advice Act (1949, UK): This landmark legislation established the Legal Aid and Advice Scheme in the United Kingdom, providing legal assistance to individuals who could not afford legal representation in civil and criminal cases.

Legal Services Corporation Act (1974, USA): In the United States, this federal law created the Legal Services Corporation (LSC), which funds legal aid programs across the country to provide legal assistance to low-income individuals in civil matters.

Legal Services Authorities Act (1987, India): This legislation established legal services authorities at the national, state, and district levels in India, tasked with providing free legal aid to marginalized and disadvantaged groups to ensure equal access to justice.

Legal Aid, Sentencing, and Punishment of Offenders Act (2012, UK): This act introduced significant reforms to the legal aid system in the UK, including changes to eligibility criteria and funding arrangements for legal aid services.

These laws represent significant milestones in the development of legal aid, reflecting a growing recognition of the importance of ensuring access to justice for all members of society, regardless of socioeconomic status.

Q.11. Discuss the provisions regarding appointment of Arbitrators under the Arbitration and Conciliation Act 1996.

Ans. The Arbitration and Conciliation Act, 1996, governs the appointment of arbitrators in India. The provisions regarding the appointment of arbitrators are outlined in Sections 11 and 12 of the Act:

Section 11 - Appointment by the Court:

If parties fail to agree on the appointment of arbitrators, or if the agreed procedure fails, either party may request the Chief Justice of the relevant High Court or the Supreme Court to appoint an arbitrator.

The Chief Justice may appoint a sole arbitrator or a panel of arbitrators, depending on the complexity of the dispute.

When appointing arbitrators, the Chief Justice must consider the qualifications and experience required for the arbitrator(s) to fairly and efficiently resolve the dispute.

The appointment process must be completed within 30 days, unless an extension is granted.

Section 12 - Impartiality and Independence:

Arbitrators must be impartial and independent throughout the arbitration process.

They should disclose any circumstances that may give rise to justifiable doubts about their impartiality or independence.

Parties are entitled to challenge an arbitrator if they have valid reasons to doubt their impartiality or independence.

If a challenge is upheld, the arbitrator may be replaced, and the arbitration proceedings may continue with a new arbitrator.

These provisions aim to ensure the fair and impartial appointment of arbitrators, thereby upholding the integrity of the arbitration process and promoting confidence in the resolution of disputes through arbitration. The Act provides a robust framework for appointing arbitrators while safeguarding the rights and interests of the parties involved in the arbitration proceedings.

Q.12. What do you mean by 'Foreign Award' under Geneva Convention? What are the conditions for enforcement for an award?

Ans. The term "Foreign Award" under the Geneva Convention refers to an arbitral award made in the territory of a contracting state other than the state where recognition and enforcement are sought. The Geneva Convention on the Execution of Foreign Arbitral Awards, commonly known as the New York Convention, provides a framework for the recognition and enforcement of foreign arbitral awards.

Conditions for enforcement of a foreign award under the New York Convention include:

Reciprocity: The Convention applies only to awards made in the territory of another contracting state. Thus, enforcement is subject to reciprocity, meaning that a foreign award may be enforced only if the country where enforcement is sought is also a party to the Convention.

Arbitration Agreement: The arbitration agreement underlying the award must be valid and enforceable under the law chosen by the parties or the law of the country where the award was made.

Proper Notice: The parties to the arbitration must have received proper notice of the arbitration proceedings and must have been given an opportunity to present their case.

Public Policy: Enforcement may be refused if the recognition or enforcement of the award would be contrary to the public policy of the country where enforcement is sought.

Non-Arbitrability: The subject matter of the dispute must be capable of settlement by arbitration under the law of the country where enforcement is sought.

Foreign awards meeting these conditions are generally enforceable in accordance with the procedures set forth in the New York Convention, facilitating international commerce and the resolution of cross-border disputes through arbitration.

Q.13. The settlement made by 'Lok Adalat' has been proved as one of the very effective alternative dispute systems. Comment.

Ans. Lok Adalat, or People's Court, has emerged as a highly effective alternative dispute resolution mechanism in India. It operates on the principles of conciliation and mediation, aiming to settle disputes amicably and expeditiously outside the formal court system. The effectiveness of Lok Adalat can be attributed to several factors:

Speedy Resolution: Lok Adalats provide a swift resolution to disputes, often resolving cases in a single sitting. This expeditious process helps alleviate the backlog of cases in traditional courts, contributing to the efficient administration of justice.

Cost-Effectiveness: Participation in Lok Adalats is usually free of cost or involves nominal fees, making it accessible to economically disadvantaged individuals who may not afford the expenses associated with traditional litigation.

Informal Atmosphere: Lok Adalats operate in an informal setting, fostering open communication and collaboration between parties. This relaxed atmosphere encourages parties to express their concerns and interests freely, facilitating the negotiation and settlement process.

Binding Settlements: Settlements reached in Lok Adalats are legally binding and enforceable as decrees of civil courts. This provides parties with a sense of certainty and finality, promoting compliance with the terms of the settlement.

Promotion of Justice: Lok Adalats uphold the principles of fairness, equity, and impartiality, ensuring that disputes are resolved in a just and equitable manner. They prioritize the interests of all parties involved, striving to achieve mutually acceptable solutions.

Lok Adalats have proven to be an effective mechanism for resolving disputes, particularly in cases involving civil, family, and petty criminal matters. Their ability to deliver timely, cost-effective, and fair resolutions has earned them widespread recognition and acceptance as a valuable component of India's justice delivery system.

ADR 2019 Question Paper

Q.1. Setting aside an award.

Ans. Setting aside an arbitral award refers to the legal process through which a party seeks to challenge the validity or enforceability of the award. This may occur if there are grounds for annulment or if the award was improperly obtained. Common grounds for setting aside an arbitral award include procedural irregularities, lack of jurisdiction, or violation of public policy. The procedure for setting aside an award varies depending on the applicable arbitration law or rules, and it typically involves filing an application or petition with the relevant court or arbitration institution within a specified time frame following the issuance of the award.

Q.2. Administrative Assistance.

Ans. Administrative assistance in air refers to the support provided by government agencies or administrative bodies to ensure the effective regulation and management of air-related activities. This assistance may include drafting and enforcing regulations, issuing permits or licenses for air-related operations, conducting inspections and audits to monitor compliance with environmental standards, and providing technical expertise and resources for air quality monitoring and improvement initiatives. Administrative assistance plays a crucial role in promoting sustainable air management practices, reducing pollution, and safeguarding public health and the environment from the adverse effects of air pollution.

Q.3. Arbitration Agreement.

Ans. An arbitration agreement is a legally binding contract between parties involved in a dispute, wherein they agree to resolve their disagreements through arbitration rather than litigation. This agreement outlines the scope of the arbitration process, including the selection of arbitrators, procedural rules, and the governing law. By entering into an arbitration agreement, parties choose to resolve their disputes in a private, impartial forum, with the arbitrator's decision being final and binding. Arbitration agreements are commonly found in commercial contracts, construction contracts, employment agreements, and other business arrangements, offering parties flexibility, confidentiality, and efficiency in dispute resolution.

Q.4. What do you mean by termination of 'Arbitration Proceedings'?

Ans. Termination of arbitration proceedings refers to the conclusion of the arbitration process before a final award is rendered. This may occur due to various reasons such as settlement between the parties, withdrawal of claims, procedural irregularities, lack of jurisdiction, or other legal grounds. Upon termination, the arbitration proceedings cease, and the parties may pursue alternative dispute resolution methods or seek recourse through the courts if necessary. Terminating arbitration proceedings ensures that disputes are resolved efficiently and effectively, while also upholding the principles of fairness and justice in dispute resolution.

Q.5. What is the difference between Arbitrator and Referee?

Ans. The main difference between an arbitrator and a referee lies in their roles and functions within the dispute resolution process. An arbitrator is a neutral third party appointed by the parties to adjudicate their dispute and render a final and binding decision, known as an arbitral award. In contrast, a referee typically acts as an expert or advisor appointed by a court or tribunal to provide technical or specialized knowledge on specific issues related to the case. While both may assist in resolving disputes, an arbitrator has the authority to make a final decision, whereas a referee's role is advisory in nature.

Q.6. Who is a Conciliator? How is he appointed?

Ans. A conciliator is a neutral third party appointed to facilitate the resolution of disputes between parties through conciliation. Unlike an arbitrator, a conciliator does not impose a decision but rather assists the parties in reaching a mutually acceptable settlement. The conciliator facilitates communication, identifies areas of agreement, and helps the parties explore potential solutions to their dispute.

The appointment of a conciliator typically occurs through mutual agreement between the parties or as provided for in a pre-existing contract or agreement. Alternatively, in some cases, the appointment may be made by a court or a designated administrative body. The conciliator's impartiality, neutrality, and expertise in conflict resolution are essential qualities for effectively assisting parties in reaching a resolution.

Q.7. What is international Commercial Arbitration?

Ans. International commercial arbitration refers to the process of resolving disputes arising from international commercial transactions through arbitration. It involves parties from different countries or jurisdictions who have entered into a contract or agreement containing an arbitration clause specifying arbitration as the chosen method of dispute resolution.

International commercial arbitration offers several advantages, including flexibility, confidentiality, and neutrality, making it a preferred choice for resolving cross-border disputes. The arbitration proceedings are typically conducted in accordance with internationally recognized arbitration rules, such as the UNCITRAL Arbitration Rules or the rules of leading arbitral institutions like the ICC or the LCIA.

The arbitral award issued at the conclusion of the proceedings is generally enforceable in multiple jurisdictions under the New York Convention, providing parties with greater certainty and predictability in the enforcement of their rights. International commercial arbitration plays a crucial role in promoting international trade and investment by offering parties an efficient and effective means of resolving their disputes.

Q.8. What is the Geneva Convention Award?

Ans. A Geneva Convention award refers to an arbitral award rendered in accordance with the Convention on the Recognition and Enforcement of Foreign Arbitral Awards, commonly known as the New York Convention or the Geneva Convention. This convention, adopted in 1958, aims to facilitate the recognition and enforcement of arbitral awards made in other contracting states.

Under the Geneva Convention, arbitral awards issued in one contracting state are generally recognized and enforceable in other contracting states, subject to limited grounds for refusal set out in the convention. These grounds typically include issues such as incapacity of parties, invalidity of the arbitration agreement, or contravention of public policy.

The Geneva Convention award provides parties involved in international commercial transactions with assurance that their arbitral awards will be respected and enforced internationally, promoting confidence in the efficacy of international arbitration as a means of dispute resolution and facilitating cross-border commerce.

Q.9. Discuss the meaning and field of "Alternate Dispute Resolution System". What is the importance of it now-a-days?

Ans. The Alternate Dispute Resolution (ADR) system encompasses various methods of resolving disputes outside of traditional courtroom litigation. These methods include negotiation, mediation, arbitration, conciliation, and others. ADR offers parties more flexibility, confidentiality, and control over the resolution process compared to litigation. It is widely used in a variety of fields, including commercial transactions, employment disputes, family law matters, and community conflicts.

The importance of ADR in contemporary society stems from several factors. Firstly, ADR promotes efficiency by offering faster and less costly resolution mechanisms compared to traditional litigation, which often involves lengthy court proceedings and significant legal expenses. Additionally, ADR allows parties to preserve relationships and maintain confidentiality, making it particularly beneficial in sensitive or ongoing business relationships where privacy is paramount. ADR promotes access to justice by providing alternative avenues for resolving disputes, especially for individuals or organizations with limited financial resources or those facing barriers to accessing the formal court system. It also helps alleviate the burden on overloaded court dockets, allowing judicial resources to be allocated more effectively to cases that require adjudication.

ADR promotes flexibility and creativity in resolving disputes, as parties have the autonomy to tailor solutions that meet their specific needs and interests. This can lead to more durable and mutually satisfactory outcomes compared to rigid court-imposed judgments.

The ADR system plays a crucial role in modern society by offering parties effective, efficient, and accessible means of resolving disputes outside of traditional litigation, thereby contributing to the administration of justice and the promotion of peaceful conflict resolution.

Q.10. On what grounds the appointment of an arbitrator can be challenged? What is the procedure to be adopted for it?

Ans. the grounds for challenging the appointment of an arbitrator are primarily governed by the Arbitration and Conciliation Act, 1996. The Act provides specific grounds on which the appointment of an arbitrator can be challenged, as well as the procedure for doing so.

Grounds for challenging the appointment of an arbitrator under the Arbitration and Conciliation Act include:

Lack of impartiality or independence: If circumstances exist that give rise to justifiable doubts as to the arbitrator's impartiality or independence.

Inability to perform duties: If the arbitrator becomes unable to perform his or her functions or fails to act without undue delay.

Failure to meet qualifications: If the arbitrator does not possess the qualifications agreed upon by the parties or required by law.

Breach of procedure: If the arbitrator fails to conduct the arbitration proceedings in accordance with the procedure agreed upon by the parties or prescribed by the Act.

The procedure for challenging the appointment of an arbitrator under the Arbitration and Conciliation Act involves submitting a written statement of the reasons for the challenge to the arbitral tribunal within 15 days of becoming aware of the constitution of the arbitral tribunal or the relevant circumstances giving rise to the challenge. The tribunal, or if it is unable to act, the relevant court, will then decide on the challenge. If the challenge is upheld, the arbitrator's appointment may be revoked, and a new arbitrator may be appointed according to the procedure agreed upon by the parties or as prescribed by the Act.

Q.11. What do you mean by Lok-Adalat? The settlement made by Lok-adalat is one of the effective Alternative Dispute System (ADR). Comment.

Ans. Lok Adalat, which translates to "People's Court," is a forum for resolving disputes through conciliation and mediation, primarily in India. It is a form of Alternative Dispute Resolution (ADR) where disputes pending before regular courts or those not yet filed in courts can be settled amicably.

Lok Adalats are organized by State Legal Services Authorities, District Legal Services Authorities, or Taluk Legal Services Committees, and they comprise presiding judicial officers, legal experts, and social activists. The proceedings are informal and conducted with the aim of achieving a compromise or settlement acceptable to all parties involved.

The settlements made by Lok Adalats hold the same legal status as decrees of civil courts. They are final and binding on the parties, and no appeal lies against them in any court of law. Moreover, the settlements reached are enforceable through the execution proceedings of civil courts.

The effectiveness of Lok Adalats as an ADR mechanism lies in several factors. Firstly, they offer a speedy resolution of disputes, often on the same day they are presented, which helps in reducing the backlog of cases in traditional courts. Secondly, the process is cost-effective and informal, making it accessible to all sections of society, including those who cannot afford the expenses of prolonged litigation. Additionally, Lok Adalats encourage conciliation and compromise, fostering a spirit of reconciliation and harmony among disputing parties.

Lok Adalats have proven to be an effective ADR mechanism by providing a swift, cost-effective, and accessible means of dispute resolution, thereby contributing to the larger goal of ensuring access to justice for all.

Q.12. What are the salient features of Arbitration And Conciliation ACt, 1996? Discuss.

Ans. The Arbitration and Conciliation Act, 1996, governs arbitration proceedings in India and provides a comprehensive framework for the resolution of disputes through arbitration and conciliation. Some of its salient features are:

Scope and applicability: The Act applies to all arbitrations and conciliations taking place within India, regardless of whether the arbitration is domestic or international.

Definition of arbitration and conciliation: The Act provides clear definitions of arbitration and conciliation, distinguishing between the two methods of dispute resolution.

Minimal judicial intervention: One of the key features of the Act is the principle of minimal judicial intervention in arbitration proceedings. Courts are instructed to intervene only where necessary, such as for the appointment of arbitrators or enforcement of awards.

Appointment of arbitrators: The Act provides mechanisms for the appointment of arbitrators, including by the parties themselves or by the court in cases of disagreement or failure to appoint.

Conduct of arbitration proceedings: The Act outlines the procedure for conducting arbitration proceedings, including the presentation of evidence, examination of witnesses, and submission of arguments.

Enforceability of awards: Arbitral awards made under the Act are final and binding on the parties and can be enforced through the courts.

Recognition of international arbitration: The Act recognizes and gives effect to international arbitration agreements and foreign arbitral awards, in line with India's obligations under international treaties.

Conciliation proceedings: The Act also provides for the conduct of conciliation proceedings, allowing parties to resolve their disputes amicably with the assistance of a neutral third party.

The Arbitration and Conciliation Act, 1996, provides a robust legal framework for the resolution of disputes through arbitration and conciliation, promoting efficiency, flexibility, and party autonomy in the resolution of disputes.

Q.13. What provisions exist in the Act for making any correction, interpretation and amendment of an award? Explain.

Ans. The Arbitration and Conciliation Act, 1996, provides provisions for making corrections, interpretations, and amendments to arbitral awards under certain circumstances. These provisions ensure that any errors or ambiguities in the award can be rectified without undermining the finality and binding nature of the award. The relevant provisions are:

Correction and interpretation of awards (Section 33):

Any party to the arbitration may request the arbitral tribunal to correct any clerical, typographical, or computational errors in the award within 30 days of receipt of the award.

Additionally, a party may request the tribunal to give an interpretation of a specific point or part of the award.

The tribunal must consider such requests promptly and make the necessary corrections or interpretations within 30 days of receiving the request.

Additional award (Section 33A):

If the arbitral tribunal omits to decide any claim or issue submitted to it or fails to provide reasons for its decision on any claim or issue, either party may, within 30 days of receipt of the award, request the tribunal to make an additional award.

The tribunal must consider the request and, if satisfied, make the additional award within 60 days from the receipt of the request.

These provisions ensure that any inadvertent errors or omissions in the arbitral award can be rectified promptly, and any ambiguities can be clarified to avoid disputes or challenges to the enforceability of the award. However, it is essential to note that these provisions do not allow parties to seek a review or reconsideration of the merits of the award but are limited to correcting procedural or clerical errors and providing interpretations where necessary.